the gut
health
cookbook

# the gut health cookbook

**Feel better from the inside out with over 60 recipes for digestive health and vitality**

Dunja Gulin

photography by Toby Scott

RYLAND PETERS & SMALL
LONDON • NEW YORK

**Designer** Manisha Patel
**Commissioning Editor** Nathan Joyce
**Head of Production** Patricia Harrington
**Art Director** Leslie Harrington
**Editorial Director** Julia Charles
**Publisher** Cindy Richards

**Photographer** Toby Scott
**Photographer's Assistant** Benjamin Wisely
**Prop Stylist** Jo Harris
**Food Stylist** Lizzie Harris

**Indexer** Vanessa Bird

Originally published in 2015 as
*Fermented Foods for Vitality & Health*
This revised edition published in 2018
by Ryland Peters & Small,
20–21 Jockey's Fields,
London WC1R 4BW
and
341 East 116th St
New York NY 10029

www.rylandpeters.com

Text © Dunja Gulin 2015, 2018
Design and photographs © Ryland Peters & Small
2015, 2018

ISBN: 978–1–84975–970–0

A CIP record for this book is available from the
British Library.

US Library of Congress cataloging–in–publication data
has been applied for.

10 9 8 7 6 5 4 3 2 1

Printed and bound in China

# Contents

# INTRODUCTION

Throughout history across our planet, different cultures and civilizations have used fermentation as a way of preserving perishable foods that would not last in the warmer weather conditions. This is the practical aspect of fermentation: by exposing foods to microorganisms in specific conditions, vegetables, meats, milk and other foods could be preserved for longer periods of time without spoilage.

I was lucky enough to grow up in a family of fermentation enthusiasts and in a culture (so to speak!) where fermentation was, and still is, a popular method of food preparation. Even those families who moved to the cities and live in apartments still make sauerkraut, storing the barrel of fermenting cabbage under their kitchen table to keep it warm and bubbly. Making yogurt and kefir in the area between Eastern Europe bordering with Mediterranean, where I come from, was something many people practised in the 1980s. I was drinking home-made kefir earlier than I could understand what it was. I definitely wasn't aware that it was the most beneficial probiotic beverage I could consume; I liked the taste and that was the only thing that mattered to me as a kid!

In the early 1990s, my dad brought home our new pet: the kombucha 'mushroom', i.e. kombucha starter culture. I regarded it as one of our pets because it needed regular feeding (same as our cats) and was growing in front of our eyes! (My mother wasn't very impressed, though). Most people do not have experience with fermentation from an early age, but it's never too late to start fermenting and enjoy all the health benefits of fermented foods. So roll up your sleeves and join me on this amazing adventure!

**About this cookbook**

To share the knowledge and experience of fermentation has been a dream of mine for a long time, but I never really thought it would come true. Fermentation was, and still is, quite niche, even though I have witnessed a growing interest in this subject in the last couple of years. My approach is influenced by the culture I come from – partially based on the European fermenting traditions, at least when it comes to fermenting vegetables. However, fermentation is universal, and microbial cultures migrate in people's suitcases (mine especially!) all over the world, so most ingredients used in this cookbook should be available everywhere.

While writing the first outline, I envisaged a cookbook that would focus on tried-and-tested recipes involving fermented foods that are suitable for preparation in a domestic kitchen. As in all my other cookbooks, the most important chapter is this one, the introduction,

as well as the chapter on basic fermentation methods, because they offer essential information on starter cultures called SCOBYS (Symbiotic Colonies of Bacteria and Yeasts) and the health benefits of fermented foods. I find that this fundamental knowledge is vital in developing the creativity one needs to be able to produce his/her own recipes later on. There are so many recipes out there to choose from and you can easily get confused and overwhelmed if you don't understand the basic principles first.

There are some great fermentation books on the market (see pages 154–155) that highlight interesting concepts and offer recipe ideas. For a beginner, though, it is difficult to start with abstract concepts without first gaining some experience of delicious, well-tested recipes that will give people the courage to explore further.

So, to sum it all up, my goal in writing this book is to help you understand the basics of fermentation, offer you exact recipes that will help you create tasty drinks, milk, grain, bean, seed and nut ferments, and to explain in detail how different microbial communities need to be cared for. I believe that this approach will help you gain confidence in order to create your own recipes. When that takes place, the sky is the limit! Get ready to unleash a real fermenting and cooking genius that lives within you!

# WHAT IS FERMENTATION?

Fermentation is the conversion of carbohydrates to alcohols and carbon dioxide or organic acids using yeasts, bacteria or both, under anaerobic conditions (i.e. without the presence of oxygen).

The term 'fermentation' is sometimes used to refer specifically to the chemical conversion of sugars into ethanol – a process which is used to produce alcoholic beverages such as wine, beer and cider. Fermentation is also employed in the leavening of bread (carbon dioxide is produced by the action of yeast as it eats up and breaks down sugars); in preservation techniques to produce lactic acid in sour foods such as sauerkraut, kimchi and yogurt; and in pickling of foods with vinegar (acetic acid). Doesn't sound too complicated, right? To translate the definition in the first sentence to more everyday, friendlier language: you take sugar-containing foods (carbohydrates) and you expose them to bacteria and/or yeasts under conditions involving no oxygen, and they will happily feed on the sugars, digesting them into alcohol, carbon dioxide, lactic acid, acetic acid, etc.

Fermentation preserves food because the organisms that are being cultivated do not allow the growth of other bacteria that would otherwise spoil the food. Also, the presence of the metabolic products of bacteria and yeasts mentioned above help to keep a selective environment that stops the growth of unwanted organisms and supports preservation of food that is being fermented.

**Starter cultures and where to get them**

Some starter cultures can be created from scratch, such as sourdough starter (see pages 36–37) but you will need to invest a little time (and sometimes a little money) to obtain your starters. In this cookbook I'm using the starter cultures that are easy to find, either by purchasing them in-store or online, or by looking for local fermented-cultures-exchange groups via social media, or by asking people on fermentation support forums. Finding someone who is willing to give or sell a starter culture is getting easier and easier. Since most SCOBYs (Symbiotic Colonies of Bacteria and Yeast) reproduce really quickly, people are looking for others to take the surplus and are often particularly grateful when somebody does! At the end of the day, you can always email me (chef@rentajchefa.com) and I'll be happy either to send you my starters or help you find someone closer to you who has them. It's a small world, after all!

The starter cultures that I've used in recipes in this cookbook are: yogurt starter, milk kefir grains, water kefir grains, kombucha, ginger beer plant and sourdough starter. My feeling is that these starters are easy enough to handle and do not require special equipment or very long periods of time to ferment into the end product. I decided that home cheese-making, culturing fish and meat, making miso and tempeh, beer brewing and winemaking are all beyond the scope of this cookbook; there are so many good-quality manuals, cookbooks and guides from people with much more knowledge and experience on those subjects, and I'm happy to stick to the fermentation methods I know well and practise in my daily life.

Maybe it isn't a good idea to get all the starter cultures I've mentioned at once. My advice for you would be to obtain one starter and allow yourself time to get to know it. Look through my recipes and choose which recipes you find most interesting. Then check what you need to make them. Once you feel confident and happy about the results of consuming the end product, choose another starter to adopt. You might end up with five starters at some point; why not? On the other hand, if you prefer beginning with vegetable ferments, you won't even need to buy starter cultures at first.

After a while, as you get more experience, you will know which ferments agree with you and are worthy of your care, and which are not.

Starter cultures are all different, the same as we are! You need to find those starters and fermentation methods that you feel you 'clicked' with, and when that happens, you will live happily ever after!

You also have to understand that each batch of kombucha, kefir, etc. will be different, so do not expect to make the same product twice. You can use the same ingredients each time and follow the recipe exactly; however, you won't be able to influence variables like the weather, the air, the water, etc. Also, written instructions are sometimes insufficient; a recipe cannot possibly include all the little details that you will witness in practice. Culturing isn't uniform; far from it, in fact! It makes sense to follow the rules, but at one point you will come to accept the unpredictability of it all and appreciate it.

After you feel you have more or less mastered the basic recipes, it's a good idea to attend a fermentation course or ask a fermentation expert for advice in case you have any doubts. Or you could always email me, of course!

**Note: Fermented foods used in the recipes in this book are denoted in bold in the ingredients lists.**

# FREQUENTLY ASKED QUESTIONS

Fermentation courses are now constantly on my calendar; I teach public and private classes and one-to-one fermentation lessons, and people constantly send me photos of their 'babies' and inform me on how the fermentation made their life richer and healthier. It's so rewarding! A set of questions arises repeatedly during every fermentation workshop (or a couple of days after), and now I have put together a Q+A that I give out to all my course participants to answer the most common questions and doubts they might have about fermented foods. I'm sharing them here, too.

**Do I need any special equipment for fermenting?**
The simple answer is no. For simple techniques of fermenting vegetables you only need a cutting board, a sharp knife, a couple of jars and unrefined salt. Jars are inexpensive to buy, re-usable and are needed for other types of fermentation. A plastic mesh strainer is a must for straining SCOBYs. It's nice to have a pickle press since it will make your life easier, but it's not absolutely necessary, since a small plate that fits into the jar and something heavy to weigh down the veggies do the job almost as well as a pickle press.

Graters, crocks, pounding tools, bottles, bowls, lids, rubber bands, a funnel, wooden chopsticks and wooden spoons are all very welcome and are usually part of home-kitchen equipment anyway. Digital kitchen scales are very useful, too. A thermometer is helpful if you plan on making a lot of yogurt, and an electric or hand-turned grain mill is a very valuable piece of equipment if you intend to use sourdough starter regularly in baking, since freshly ground flour is so much richer in enzymes than store-bought. But then again, it's not absolutely necessary! Don't wait until you have all the fancy equipment; start making simple fermenting recipes and buy things you don't have as you go.

**Are home-fermented food and beverages safe?**
Fermentation has been the primary means of food preservation for centuries, long before every household in the Western world could afford a fridge, and long before industrialized canning became the norm for food preservation. Vinegar, pickles, kimchi, yogurt etc. are all products of acidification, either by lactic or acetic acid, in which toxins and pathogenic microorganisms cannot survive. This is what makes fermented foods safe (and even safer than raw foods) – the 'bad guys' cannot survive since there are too many 'good guys' hanging together!

However, fermented foods do have a limited shelf life, and can go bad. Spoiled fermented foods aren't good for you! Each recipe in this book will tell you how long the product can be stored before spoilage occurs. But please, rely on your common sense as well as your sense of smell and taste.

## What type of salt should I use for fermenting vegetables?

Any type of salt except table salt, which is over-refined, mineral-depleted and contains additives. This doesn't mean that fermentation won't happen if such salt is used, but it's a shame to use it. I mostly use unrefined sea salt (uniodized), and sometimes Himalayan or other types of un-refined rock salts. Fine and course salts are both OK, but fine salt does dissolve more easily.

## What is the best way to eat fermented foods to gain the maximum benefits?

To gain the maximum benefits from fermented foods, make sure you consume them uncooked, at room temperature. Cooking deactivates enzymes in foods, and that is why you have to make sure you are eating enough uncooked enzyme-rich foods every day. However, you will soon realise that you cannot possibly eat and drink it all raw! Enzyme-rich foods are also delicious when used in cooked or baked recipes, and cooked or baked fermented recipes are still

easier to digest than other types of cooked foods. So, use fermented foods in cooking to make delicious and healthy dishes, and still consume enough beneficial enzymes from your daily portion of uncooked fermented foods, so you can enjoy the best of both worlds.

## Is there any danger of cross-contamination?

In most cases, there is no need to worry about cross-contamination. All my fermenting jars and presses sit in the same pantry and I never have any problems. Contamination is only likely if you use the same utensils for different cultures. So, keep your hands, work surface and equipment clean – usually that is enough.

## What type of water is best to use?

We need to use water to make the salty brine for vegetables, to make tea for kombucha, to make sugar solution for water kefir, etc. The problem with most public water supplies is that chlorine is added to the water to kill microbes, and that same chlorine might also prevent fermentation microbes from doing their work- it depends how heavily chlorinated the water is. To remove chlorine you can either use some kind of water-filter, or you can boil the water and leave it to cool to room temperature – the chlorine will evaporate.

# HEALTH BENEFITS & HEALING REMEDIES

Fermented foods are highly nutritious and easier to digest than the same foods eaten in their raw or cooked state. They are so nutritious because beneficial microorganisms that are involved in the fermentation process add live enzymes, B vitamins and protein to the food. Fermentation also increases the bioavailability of minerals present in food, helping the body to assimilate more nutrition. The microorganisms break down complex proteins, carbohydrates and fats into more easily assimilated molecules. Therefore, since healthy gut flora plays a key role in absorption, our body is able to absorb the maximum amount of nutrients, preventing nutrient deficiencies that are so common today.

Fermented foods are highly digestible because good bacteria pre-digest the food, and also because beneficial cultures supply additional enzymes to assist with the digestive process so that our digestive system doesn't have as much work to do. So, we could say that helping digestion, absorption and adding nutrition are the most well-known health-promoting properties of fermented foods. However, since the processes of fermentation and the processes happening in our gut during digestion are so much more complex and interrelated, many other health and healing benefits happen as a consequence.

Apart from aiding digestion, the lactic-acid bacteria present in fermented foods also alter the pH in the intestines, and a balanced pH in the intestines has been associated with long life and good health. Also, the same lactic-acid bacteria create omega-3 fatty acids, essential for immune system function, which brings us to another very important health benefit of fermented foods: they strengthen our immune system! Did you know that 80 per cent of our immune system resides in the wall of the intestines? So, while enjoying a home-made probiotic soda or home-fermented kefir cream cheese spread over a slice of sourdough bread, you are actually building a resistant immune system that will help you fight disease. Even though I do not believe in miracle foods, if any type of food helps your body to function optimally, it must be fermented food!

In the era when antibiotics are so frequently prescribed and gut flora is so frequently damaged, fermented foods replenish the microflora of the digestive tract. Good bacteria also make it easier for our bodies to get rid of toxins from food and the environment, and function as free-radical scavengers. Some types of fermentation (e.g. soaking grains, beans, seeds, nuts etc.) neutralizes toxins (eg. phytic acid) that would otherwise interfere with, and block, the absorption of nutrients during digestion.

Improved digestion brings many other benefits, such as digestive comfort, regular bowel movement, better sleeping, healthy and radiant skin, increased energy levels, loss of excess weight, possible decrease of sugar cravings, normalization of blood pressure levels, acid reflux and heartburn control, decrease of inflammation in the bloodstream, and candida-overgrowth control, among other things. While all this might sound amazing and the answer to many of our health problems, I have to remind you that we are all different, and while a cup of kefir a day might help in controlling the acid reflux for one person, it might not be so effective for somebody else. That is why it is important to include many different types of fermented foods and beverages into our diet, and see for ourselves which of them agree with us and which do not.

Treatments that help people heal naturally are present in all cultures. Not all of those treatments include fermented foods, but there are some that do, and many of those come from Japan. I was lucky to have been exposed to some of that knowledge through macrobiotic philosophy during my studies, and I have to say that the remedies that I learned to make really work, and have proven their effectiveness many times! I much prefer preparing an unusual hot drink containing umeboshi plum than taking a medicine for a headache or an upset stomach, and I'm always eager to do everything in my power to get better or help somebody else get better naturally, before heading to the doctor.

There are a number of fermented foods that are used as remedies. Umeboshi plum is a Japanese speciality; it is a sour and salty fermented fruit that is usually referred to as a plum, but is actually a pickled apricot. It is a very popular *tsukemono* (pickle) in Japan, served mostly with rice. It has been used for centuries to treat a wide variety of health complaints; it's highly alkaline, good for digestion and the prevention of nausea and is known for its detoxifying properties, while it also acts as an antibacterial agent. Adding umeboshi to rice seems to inhibit bacteria and acts as a preservative.

Miso, a thick paste produced by the fermentation of soybeans/soya beans, takes months or even years to mature, and the lengthy aging acts as an external digestive system, making it much easier for humans to digest. Miso is full of natural digestive enzymes, lactic acid-forming bacteria, salt-resistant yeasts and microorganisms that digest complex proteins. It's also very rich in mineral antioxidants and phytonutrients and plays an important role in maintaining and strengthening the immune system.

# Spring onion & miso tea

As soon as you notice the first symptoms of a cold, make yourself a cup of this hot and salty tea. Miso will nourish you and alkalize your blood, and spring onion/scallion will boost circulation and increase sweating. Adding a little ginger juice just before drinking makes this tea even more powerful.

**1 teaspoon hatcho miso**
240 ml/1 cup just-boiled water
2 spring onions/scallions,
    finely chopped
small piece of fresh ginger
    (optional)

Serves 1

Dilute the miso in 2 tablespoons of just-boiled water. Add the spring onions/scallions and the remaining hot water. Grate the ginger, if using, and squeeze a few drops of juice in the tea. Stir and drink hot in small sips. Chew the onion well. If you don't have spring onions/scallions, use onion or leek. Hatcho miso is the most strengthening type of miso made out of soybeans/soy beans, salt and koji starter, but other darker types, like miso pastes with added barley or rice can be used instead if you have no soy miso at hand.

# Ume-sho-kuzu drink

This healing drink is one of the most well-known Japanese-style remedies, and it is made using umeboshi plum, shoyu (Japanese natural soy sauce) and kuzu thickener (starch from a wild mountain root vegetable). I have already discussed the role of the umeboshi plum in detail so it's not at all surprising that it has a star role here. It's magic in a cup, directly from nature!

**½ umeboshi plum, stoned/pitted**
240 ml/1 cup water
1 teaspoon kuzu or arrowroot
few drops of shoyu
few drops of freshly squeezed
    ginger juice (optional)

Serves 1

Finely chop the umeboshi plum, place in a small saucepan and cover with the water. Bring to a slow boil and simmer for around 4 minutes. Dilute the kuzu or arrowroot in 2–3 teaspoons of cold water, add it to the saucepan, whisking constantly to avoid clumping, and simmer briefly until the liquid becomes translucent. Add the shoyu, let simmer for another 30 seconds and remove from the heat. Squeeze in a few drops of freshly squeezed ginger juice (if using), especially if you are trying to fight nausea or a stuffy nose.

Sip while hot and make a fresh portion each time. Drink 2–3 times per day for a couple of days. However, even 1 cup can make a big difference! Remember that all ingredients (except fresh ginger) have an almost indefinite shell life so make sure you visit your local health-food store and buy the ingredients to have them at hand whenever needed!

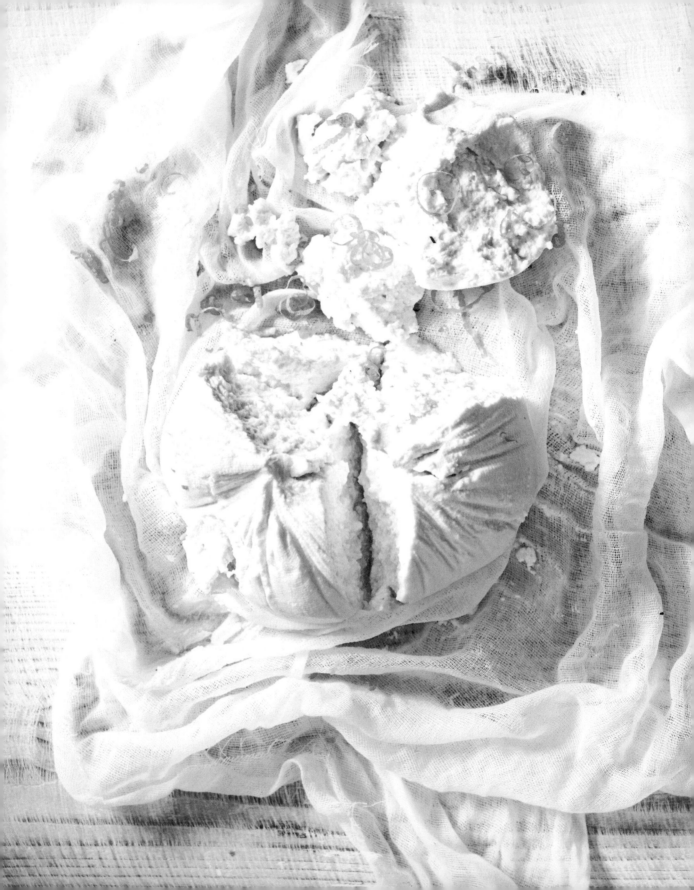

chapter one

# basic fermentation methods

# How to make yogurt and vegan yogurt

You don't need any special equipment to make yogurt at home, just a little patience. I make both milk yogurt and vegan soya/soy yogurt (made with soya/soy milk and soya/soy yogurt) – they are different in taste and texture but equally delicious! First, try to find a good yogurt starter (live-culture yogurts, which are readily available from local health-food stores). You can also buy store-bought yogurts as starters, but you will need to buy a new one for every third batch or so, because the laboratory-derived cultures are not as strong and stable as traditional cultures. The quality of milk is also important. To make a thick and tasty yogurt, use organic (not ultra-pasteurized) whole milk, and if using soya milk/soy milk, use the best-quality, organic, unsweetened kind you can find. If you are making yogurt in the long term, I suggest sourcing a supplier (online or locally) of traditional yogurt culture, because it will serve you for many years without losing its effectiveness – you just take a small amount of the yogurt you just made and use it as a starter for the next batch.

Make sure that the starter is at room temperature. Pour the milk into a heavy-bottomed saucepan and heat gently and slowly, whisking frequently, until it starts forming small bubbles. If you have a cooking thermometer, it should read 80°C (175°F). Allow the milk to cool to 45°C (115°F). If you haven't got a cooking thermometer, dip your finger in the milk; if it's fairly warm but not hot, it's about right.

Whisk in the starter until fully dissolved. Yogurt cultures need warmth to grow so you need to keep the mixture of milk and starter warm for 6–12 hours in order for the milk to thicken into a creamy yogurt.

Pour the mixture into warm glass jars (heat them in the oven beforehand for 10 minutes at 100°C/210°F), seal and keep in a warm place (ideally at 40–45°C/105°–115°F) for 6–12 hours. What I do is place filled jars in a thermal bag and wrap the bag in a blanket, or heat the oven to 60°C (140°F), put the jars inside the oven, switch off the heat leaving the oven light on, and maintain a constant temperature by checking from time to time and putting the oven on for a couple of minutes, if necessary. If the temperature is too high, the starter cultures will die, and if it's too low it will take much longer for the yogurt to ferment, making a very runny and mild yogurt drink. All this may seem complicated, but it's just a matter of finding a way to keep the temperature constant and waiting for the starter cultures to do their job. Refrigerate and enjoy! Your home-made yogurt will keep for 5–6 days.

1 litre/4 cups whole milk or unsweetened soya milk/soy milk

60 ml/¼ cup live-culture, plain regular yogurt or soya/soy yogurt or 1–2 tablespoons traditional yogurt culture

Makes 1 kg/4 cups

# How to make water kefir

Water kefir grains are another SCOBY (see page 8), which feed on sugary water or juice and produce a fizzy liquid rich in probiotics. These small translucent granules (sometimes also referred to as tibicos), consist of lactic-acid bacteria and some yeasts, and are actually distinctly different from milk kefir grains, even though they share the same name. Like any symbiotic community of bacteria and yeast, water kefir granules need regular feeding in order to survive. I use raw cane sugar, rice syrup, maple syrup or honey diluted in water to feed them, but they will also thrive on agave syrup or any

other carbohydrate sweetener, or on any sweet liquid (like fruit juice, coconut water, nut milks, etc.). Granulated white sugar can also be used, but you'll need to add a pinch of unrefined sea salt to help the water kefir ferment effectively. If you or your family members are big soft drink/soda fans, and want to avoid unhealthy commercial drinks, you can make your own fermented probiotic soft drinks with the help of the water kefir grains. Depending on the sweetener and fruit used, you can make many kinds of soft drink/soda and enjoy the health benefits at the same time!

**4 tablespoons water kefir grains**

**100 g/½ cup raw cane sugar or other sweetener**

**1 litre/4 cups water, preferably non-chlorinated**

2 x 1.5-litre/quart jars with tightly fitting lids

plastic strainer

wooden or plastic spoon

Makes 1 litre/4 cups

Put the water kefir grains in the jar, add the sweetener and water and stir well. Cover it loosely or seal with the jar lid (I prefer sealing the jar to get more fizziness). Keep the jar away from direct sunlight and leave to ferment for 48 hours, stirring it on a couple of occasions during that time. Taste the liquid – it should taste slightly sour. If it's still sweet, leave it to ferment for another 12–24 hours (this might be necessary in winter or when your kitchen temperature is lower than 20°C/68°F). Strain the liquid into a clean jar or bottle, and repeat the feeding process.

This fermented drink can be enjoyed immediately or refrigerated. If you are going to put it in the fridge, it's best to consume it within around 1 week. To create different flavour sodas, see the Probiotic Drinks chapter.

# How to make milk kefir

Kefir grains are combinations of yeast and bacteria. They are active, alive and unique and cannot be created in the laboratory. Milk kefir grains feed on lactose and therefore need milk sugar to survive. Since they eat lactose, milk kefir is almost lactose-free, rich in beneficial bacteria and much easier to digest than unfermented milk. I am lucky enough to have a neighbour who herds goats, so I pick up fresh goat's milk every other evening to feed my kefir grains and they thrive on it! But store-bought whole cow's milk can also be used with great results. The greater the fat content, the creamier the kefir.

Put the kefir grains in the jar. Pour over the milk. Cover the jar with a paper towel or clean muslin/cheesecloth and fix it with a rubber band, or if you want the kefir to be fizzy, tighten the lid. Let rest for 18–24 hours, stirring occasionally. The exact time of fermentation depends on the outside temperature and the strength of the grains. If whey separates from the kefir, it has been fermenting for too long, but that's also OK – just shake it. Strain the kefir from the grains using a non-metal strainer and refrigerate. Or, if the kefir grains have formed big clusters, pick them out with wooden chopsticks. Kefir will thicken slightly with cooling. It will keep in the fridge for weeks!

Place the grains in a clean jar, covering them with another 240 ml/1 cup of milk and repeat the process. The grains will grow and multiply, and after a couple of days you will need to increase the amount of milk and eventually give away some of your grains. For example, I started with 1 teaspoon of grains and 1 cup of milk and within a month I had 1 cup of big kefir lumps and was fermenting about 1.5 litres/6 cups of milk daily! Eventually I had to start giving away some kefir grains, because I didn't want to make more milk kefir than we could use in a day.

Always use clean utensils and jars, do not expose the grains to high heat, feed them regularly and avoid using any metal equipment when handling kefir grains. If you're taking a short holiday/vacation, put the grains in 240 ml/1 cup of milk and refrigerate for up to 10 days before the next feeding. Enjoy kefir on its own, as a nourishing and refreshing drink, or use it in raw, cooked and baked recipes – I'm offering you many kefir recipes in this book!

1 tablespoon kefir grains
**240 ml/1 cup cow's/goat's milk, at room temperature**
720-ml/24-fl. oz. glass jar
plastic or nylon mesh strainer
paper towel or muslin/cheesecloth
rubber band

Makes 240 ml/1 cup

# How to make rejuvelac

Apart from being a fermented liquid which helps to start the fermentation process of other foods (e.g. seeds and nuts for making cheese), rejuvelac is also a great energizing drink, so you can make more and enjoy it as an enzyme-rich refreshment when you need a boost.

Put the spelt berries and water in a jar, cover with a paper towel or muslin/cheesecloth, and store in a warm place for 48 hours, or until fizzy and a little sour. In summer, you can just leave it on a work surface, but in winter you'll need to put it close to a radiator or oven. You can let it ferment at room temperature in winter, but it will take at least a week.

Drain, keep the liquid and discard the berries. Try using rye berries, unhulled millet, buckwheat, even brown rice instead of spelt berries.

30 g/¼ cup sprouted spelt berries
(a tiny white tail is enough)
480 ml/2 cups water

Makes 480 ml/2 cups

# How to make yogurt and kefir cream cheese

One cup of this delicious and velvety cream cheese calls for 1.2 litres/5 cups of yogurt or milk kefir, which might seem a lot, but it's worth it! My advice is to purchase a cotton straining bag (used for making tofu or nut milks) because muslin/cheesecloth isn't woven tightly enough to divide cream cheese from whey. You'll find that home-made cream cheese is far superior in texture and taste to its store-bought counterparts!

**1.2 litres/5 cups Yogurt (see pages 18–19) or Milk Kefir (see pages 22–23)**

tightly woven cotton straining bag

Makes 240 g/1 cup

Put a large sieve/strainer over a large bowl. Place the straining bag in the sieve/strainer and pour the yogurt or milk kefir into the bag.

Fold the top of the bag so that the cream cheese cannot leak out, cover with something heavy (a bowl, a stone or a measuring weight) and allow the whey to drain off for 8–12 hours, or longer. During the summer months I leave it to drain in the fridge, to avoid over-fermentation.

Keep the whey for other recipes, and serve the cream cheese as it is or add herbs/spices (see pages 94 and 97) or triple this recipe and make the delicious Austrian-style Cheesecake (see pages 142–143). This cheese can keep in the fridge for a week, if not longer. Enjoy its creaminess and the fact that you made it all by yourself!

# How to make plant-based cream cheese

Even though I enjoy good-quality sheep's or goat's milk cheeses once in a while, I find plant-based cheese equally tasty! In this recipe, Rejuvelac (see pages 24–25) acts as a culturing agent, quickens the fermentation process and contributes to the 'cheesy' taste. The result is a creamy plant-based cheese with various degrees of sharpness. The warmer the temperature and the longer the cheese cultures, the sharper it will taste. Nuts that can be used are cashews, blanched almonds and macadamia nuts, and there's also the option of combining nuts with certain seeds, most commonly sunflower seeds and possibly also pumpkin seeds. Cashews and almonds make a white cream cheese, so use them to make this recipe when serving it to sceptics and milk-cheese lovers!

270 g/2 cups unsalted cashews, soaked overnight

¼ teaspoon sea salt

2 garlic cloves, pressed

2 tablespoons olive oil

55–110 ml/¼–½ cup Rejuvelac (see pages 24–25)

muslin/cheesecloth

Makes 600 g/2½ cups

Drain the nuts and put them in a high-speed blender. Add the salt, garlic and oil and start blending, adding just enough of the rejuvelac to achieve a completely smooth texture. Use a tamper (a tool that comes with the blender used to push the ingredients down the blades) to help with this. Line a sieve/strainer with two layers of muslin/cheesecloth, spoon the mixture into the sieve/strainer, cover with the edges of the muslin/cheesecloth and let rest at room temperature (preferably warm) for 24–48 hours. Form into the desired shape (I usually just flip it over from the strainer onto a plate). Leave it covered with the muslin/cheesecloth or peel it off and wrap the plate in clingfilm/plastic wrap. Leave in the fridge to finish setting for another 24 hours before serving.

This is a soft cheese, and can sit in the fridge for about 10 days. To make a different flavoured cheese, add nutritional yeast flakes, crushed black pepper or dried/fresh herbs and spices, then line a ramekin with muslin/cheesecloth and refrigerate for a 1–2 hours to set. Flip it out of the ramekin, remove the muslin/cheesecloth and serve on a wooden cutting board. Each time you make this cheese it can look and taste different, so you won't get bored!

# How to make ginger beer

Very similar to water kefir grains, ginger beer plant, or ginger bug, is another type of SCOBY, which ferments sugary water into ginger beer. The culture is not really a plant, but rather a group of small grains, like translucent rice granules. Ginger beer plant consists of only one type of bacteria and one type of yeast living in harmony, as opposed to other types of SCOBY, which are more complex. It is capable of making drinks with a slightly higher alcohol content, such as traditionally brewed ginger beer, although it can also be used to ferment sweet drinks in the same fashion as water kefir grains.

Peel and chop the ginger into small chunks. Put 4 tablespoons of ginger beer plant in the jar, add the sweetener, lemon juice, chopped ginger and water and stir well. Cover it loosely or seal with the jar lid. Keep the jar away from direct sunlight and leave to ferment for 2 days, stirring a couple of times. Taste the liquid – it should taste slightly sour. If still sweet, leave to ferment for another 12–24 hours (this might be necessary in winter or when your kitchen temperature is lower than 20°C/68°F). Strain the liquid into a clean bottle or jar, pick out the ginger pieces in between the ginger beer plant granules and discard the ginger. Repeat the feeding process.

This drink can be enjoyed immediately or refrigerated. You can also try making a delicious (but much stronger) ginger ale (see pages 128–129).

5-cm/2-inch piece of fresh ginger root

4 tablespoons ginger beer plant or water kefir grains

100 g/½ cup raw cane sugar

freshly squeezed juice of 1 lemon

1 litre/4 cups water, preferably non-chlorinated

1.5-litre/quart preserving jar

1.5-litre/quart glass bottle (or another 1.5-litre/quart preserving jar)

Makes 1 litre/4 cups

# How to make kombucha

Kombucha is a fermented energizing drink that has gained popularity in the past 20 years, even though its beneficial properties have been enjoyed in Central and Eastern Europe for much longer. Kombucha is fermented with the help of a symbiotic colony of bacteria and yeast (SCOBY). Most kombuchas need both sugar and caffeine to survive and therefore thrive on sweetened black or green tea. To make kombucha tea at home, you can either use a small piece of kombucha mother, or you can make it out of the store-bought, live-cultured plain kombucha drink. Usually, starting the fermentation with kombucha mother is faster than with kombucha drink.

960 ml/4 cups water

2 tablespoons sencha green tea (or other green/black tea)

100 g/½ cup raw brown sugar

**small piece of kombucha mother or 480 ml/2 cups live-cultured plain kombucha drink**

1.5-litre/quart glass jar

muslin/cheesecloth or paper towel

rubber band

Makes 1.5 litres/6 cups

Bring the water to a boil, remove from the heat and add the loose tea or tea bags. Steep for around 10 minutes. Strain the tea into a clean jar, add the sugar and whisk until dissolved. Let cool to room temperature. Add the piece of kombucha mother or the kombucha drink, cover with muslin/cheesecloth or a paper towel and fix with a rubber band.

If using the mother, let it sit for about a week, then check the taste. In case it's still too sweet, let it brew for longer. If using kombucha drink, after the first week check every couple of days; a 'baby' kombucha, or skin, should start forming on the surface of the tea. The brewing time depends on the size of the kombucha piece/strength of the store-bought kombucha and temperature (in winter it will ferment much slower unless kept in a warm place).

Ferment until reaching the desired taste – you can enjoy it mildly sweet or wait a while longer for a sour, fizzy kombucha. When you're happy with the taste, transfer most of the liquid into another jar or bottle and drink or refrigerate. Carefully pour the remaining cooled fresh tea over the mother and leftover liquid. If you're going on holiday/vacation, feed the kombucha with freshly made tea and refrigerate immediately. It will need new feeding in about 30 days.

Make sure you use only clean equipment when handling kombucha. In case mould appears on the surface, or you see anything suspicious going on, throw everything away and start over with a new kombucha. Try drinking a small amount of brewed kombucha a couple of days in a row and see how you feel – some people (like me) are sensitive to stimulants like caffeine, or even the smallest amount of alcohol (usually, fermented kombucha contains up to 0.5% alcohol), so it's not a drink for everybody. However, most people enjoy drinking it and it's a much healthier alternative to coffee and tea!

# How to ferment vegetables

Out of all the fermented foods and beverages you can make at home, fermenting vegetables is the easiest type of fermentation, and a great way to enter the world of home-fermented foods! There are many different methods of fermenting vegetables across the world, but one thing is certain: whichever method you use, fermented vegetables are very nutritious, so eating them regularly will bring you many health benefits. They are also very tasty and a great addition to your everyday meals! The basic principle of most of vegetable fermenting methods is that vegetables are submerged under liquid and the bacteria native to the vegetables start the fermentation process. Lactic-acid bacteria create an acidic environment in which unwanted organisms cannot survive, protecting vegetables from spoilage. No wonder that lactic-acid fermentation has been historically popular as a food-preservation method, as it is an effective method of preserving vegetables for the colder months of the year when fresh vegetables are not always available. Eating fermented foods also protects against vitamin C deficiency and provides other critical nutrients for a well-balanced diet.

**Dry-salting** refers to adding salt to chopped vegetables, which are then squeezed or pounded until the salt pulls out the water and the vegetables start sweating. The juice that comes out of the vegetables is then used as a brine in which the vegetables are submerged during the fermentation. See Sauerkraut with Quinces (pages 76–77) and Purple Sauerkraut with Dulse & Caraway Seeds (pages 78–79) for more details.

**Brining** is more suitable for large pieces of vegetables or whole vegetables. They are not salted directly but rather submerged in brine and kept submerged, or even under pressure, for a certain period of time. Brines can also be flavoured with different spices so that the vegetables absorb the spices and become aromatic or strong-flavoured. Also, yogurt or kefir whey can be used instead of water to help the fermentation process. See recipes for Turshiya (pages 72–73), Turmeric and Chilli Kimchi (pages 112–113), and Cultured Salsa Cruda (pages 74–75) for more details.

**Fermenting in miso** is a Japanese way of pickling (called *miso-zuke* in Japanese), one of many types of Japanese preserved vegetables or *tsukemono*. Since miso is a paste, sliced or whole vegetables (most usually roots, garlic, onion, etc.) are layered with miso and completely surrounded by the paste, and left to ferment from anything between a couple of days to up to a couple of years! See recipes for Garlic Condiment and Onion Anchovies (pages 110–111) for more details.

**Fermenting with shoyu** is another *tsukemono*, and is possibly the easiest and quickest Japanese pickling technique, similar to brining. Vegetables are thinly sliced, mixed with *shoyu* (traditional soy sauce) and put under pressure for a short period of time (up to 2 hours). Vegetables remain crunchy and the taste is light and refreshing. See the recipe for Quick Radish Tsukemono (pages 80–81) for more details.

# How to make a sourdough starter

Making your own starter might seem daunting at first, but it really is very simple. Your only job is to replenish the batter with fresh water and flour once a day for about 2 weeks, and the bacteria and yeasts from your environment will do the rest! The right temperature is important to develop a good starter, so make sure you keep it in a warm spot, anywhere from 20–30°C (68–86°F) will do. Starters develop much faster and are stronger if freshly ground flour is used, because fresh flour is full of enzymes and ferments more easily. If you're not using freshly ground flour, buy high-quality organic rye flour.

1.35 kg/10⅓ cups rye flour
1.6 litres/6¾ cups water

wide-mouthed 720-ml/24-fl. oz. jar
rubber band

paper napkin

**Day 1** In a clean jar, mix 60 ml/¼ cup water with 50 g/ ⅓ cup rye flour. Cover and let sit at room temperature for 24 hours.

**Day 2** Add the same amount of rye and water to the mixture in the jar, stir well, cover and let sit at room temperature for 24 hours.

**Day 3** Repeat the procedure from day 2.

**Day 4** There should be some bubbles visible below the surface of rye batter. Leave 1 tablespoon in the jar and discard the rest. Add to the jar 120 ml/½ cup water and 100 g/¾ cup rye flour. Mix well and let sit for 24 hours.

**Day 5** Again, discard all but 1 tablespoon of the batter and add to the jar 120 ml/½ cup water and 100 g/¾ cup rye flour. Mix well and let sit for another 24 hours.

**Day 6 and 7** Repeat the same as day 5. The starter should now be bubbly and increase in volume by ⅓ after 24 hours of fermentation.

**Day 8–13** Repeat the procedure from day 5. By day 13 your starter should double in volume in 24 hours, or earlier. The batter should be full of bubbles and have a

thick layer of froth on top. These are all signs that your starter is ready for use in baking.

**Day 14** Discard all but 2 tablespoons of your starter, and feed it with 240 ml/1 cup of water and 200 g/1⅔ cups rye flour. It should double in size in 12 hours. Now you will have plenty of starter that can be used immediately for baking and you only need to save 2 tablespoons of it to keep the sourdough going. Don't forget that, because you will need to start all over again if you have no developed starter left in the jar! When you use the starter, save 2 tablespoons of it, replenish it again with 240 ml/ 1 cup water and 200 g/1⅔ cups rye flour, stir well and leave in a warm place for 12 hours or until bubbly again. If you use the starter every day to bake fresh bread, repeat this procedure every day. I use my starter once a week so I refrigerate it after the replenished starter has fermented for 12 hours and I take it out a day before I plan baking (within 1 week of placing it in the fridge), and feed it again as done on day 14. Even if you do not plan on using your starter for longer than a week, you have to keep feeding it once a week, as done on day 14, leaving it to ferment for 12 hours or until bubbly and refrigerating it again. This can go on forever!

chapter two
# Breakfast

# Omega 3-rich breakfast bowl

The typical diet in Western countries today contains far fewer omega-3 fatty acids than the human diet of a century ago, and it's not a good thing. We should try to include as many foods rich in omega-3s as we can (such as flaxseed and chia seeds, walnuts, soya beans/soybeans and tofu) because they are essential for normal metabolism.

6 tablespoons flaxseed

480 ml/2 cups Yogurt
  (see pages 18–19)

4 tablespoons chia seeds

200 g/2 very ripe bananas, peeled

fresh lemon balm, to garnish

Serves 2

To make flaxseed flour, grind the flaxseed in a high-speed blender or spice grinder into a fine flour. Do this just before consuming it, or grind it in advance and keep in a sealed jar in the fridge until you're ready to use it (it will keep for 1 week in the fridge). Do not buy pre-ground flaxseed because it loses most of its nutrients a few days after grinding and becomes rancid very quickly.

In a big bowl mix the yogurt with the flaxseed flour and chia seeds and let sit for 10 minutes, allowing the chia seeds to soften. Chop the bananas, fold in and serve. Decorate with fresh lemon balm for a refreshing green colour and a nice lemony aroma.

# Comforting cacao porridge

I grew up eating Čokolino, a wheat and chocolate cereal to which only hot milk needs to be added for a creamy porridge/oatmeal that kids (and adults) were crazy about. But it wasn't really a healthy meal – it was full of sugar and processed wheat! So I decided to create a much healthier version, with lightly fermented oats, real cacao and a good-quality sweetener – a wholesome creamy treat for both quick weekdays and lazy Sunday mornings!

Put the fine rolled oats in a jar and cover with 480 ml/2 cups of water. Cover loosely with a lid and let soak (ferment) for at least 24 hours, or longer.

Pour the soaked oats in a saucepan, add all other ingredients and whisk over a medium heat until creamy and bubbly, for about 3–5 minutes. Your porridge/oatmeal is ready!

I'd advise against making the porridge/oatmeal too sweet. I think it's better to save sweets for dessert and serve this oatmeal only mildly sweet with a kick of real cacao taste.

50 g/½ cup fine rolled oats

480 ml/2 cups water

⅛ teaspoon salt

2 tablespoons roasted ground hazelnuts or hazelnut butter

1 tablespoon raw cacao powder

3 tablespoons brown rice syrup/ high-quality maple syrup, or to taste

Serves 2

# Mineral-rich porridge

Millet is an amazing grass and grain that is highly underestimated nowadays, and we shouldn't feed it only to our canaries, but to our children as well! It is very rich in copper, phosphorus, manganese and magnesium – a veritable mountain of minerals! Serve with sunflower seeds or other seeds, and a spoonful or two of fermented vegetables or a fermented condiment, and millet porridge/oatmeal becomes a tasty, satisfying breakfast, full of nutrients.

100 g/½ cup millet

480 ml/2 cups water

**2 tablespoons yogurt whey or kefir whey (see pages 26–27)**

**½ umeboshi plum or ⅛ teaspoon salt**

**2 tablespoons dry-roasted sunflower seeds**

**1 teaspoon soy sauce**

720-ml/24-fl.oz. glass jar

muslin/cheesecloth or paper towel

rubber band

Serves 1–2

Put the millet in a sieve/strainer and wash well under running water. Drain and put in the jar. Pour over the water and add 2 tablespoons of whey. Cover with muslin/cheesecloth or a paper towel and fix with a rubber band. Let soak for 2–3 days at room temperature and stir at least once a day. The whey will speed up the fermentation process by adding enzymes. Fermenting grains this way makes them more digestible and reduces anti-nutrients (compounds that interfere with the absorption of nutrients), which has the effect of improving nutritional value.

Put the soaked millet, together with the soaking water, in a small saucepan. Bring to the boil over a medium heat. Stir occasionally to prevent burning and boiling over. Add the umeboshi plum or salt and simmer, half-covered, for about 20 minutes. Add more hot water during the cooking, if necessary, to get a creamy porridge/oatmeal.

Wash and drain the sunflower seeds (this will prevent them from burning) and dry-roast in a frying pan/skillet over a medium heat, stirring constantly until the seeds start sizzling, at which point they will release their aroma, become golden brown and puff up. Transfer to a bowl and add the soy sauce. Mix until the hot seeds absorb all the soy sauce and become dry and crunchy. Sprinkle the seeds over the warm porridge/oatmeal and serve with 1 tablespoon of Spicy Leek & Miso Condiment (see pages 114–115), Turmeric and Chilli Kimchi (see pages 112–113) or any live-cultured vegetables.

# Soft polenta with yogurt & sesame seeds

Soft polenta is the breakfast of my childhood. In my family everyone has their favourite way of serving polenta, and although my mum swears it tastes best with cold milk, and my husband eats it only with hot cocoa, I have to argue that the polenta-yogurt combination is the best! Sprinkle a spoonful of roasted and salted sesame seeds on top and enjoy! This breakfast will keep your tummy happy for many hours.

Bring the water to a boil, add the salt and slowly whisk in the polenta. Lower the heat, cover, and let cook for 15 minutes. There's no need to stir. Remove from the heat and leave it to rest, covered, for another 15 minutes. If you prefer harder polenta, use 750 ml/3 cups of water.

While the polenta is cooking, prepare the sesame seeds. Put them in a sieve/strainer and rinse quickly under running water. Drain well. Wetting sesame seeds not only rinses off possible dust, but also prevents the seeds from jumping out of your pan and from burning. Put the sesame seeds in a heavy-bottomed frying pan/skillet over a medium heat and dry-roast, stirring constantly up and down, until the seeds puff up and become golden. You can dry-roast sesame seeds in advance – stored in a sealed jar when cooled they will keep for 1 month.

Scoop the polenta onto 2 separate plates, pour over the yogurt and sprinkle with sesame seeds. Enjoy your breakfast!

840 ml/3½ cups water

½ teaspoon sea salt

170 g/1 cup coarse polenta/cornmeal

500 g/2 cups Yogurt (see pages 18–19)

4 tablespoons sesame seeds

Serves 2

# Banana & blueberry kefir muffins

These muffins are to die for – very light, juicy and happy to accommodate any fruit you might have lying around in your pantry. My favourite is fresh blueberries, but raspberries, sour cherries or a mix of forest fruits all work really well, as do chopped peaches, apricots and plums. The choice of flours is also up to you. I have used some organic coconut flour (not flakes) to lower the gluten amount, but using only unbleached flour with some wholegrain/whole-wheat flour is also an option.

Preheat the oven to 180°C (350°F) Gas 4.

If necessary, place the jar with coconut oil in a pot of hot water to melt it.

Blend the first four ingredients in an electric blender. This is the wet mixture. Sift all of the remaining ingredients (except for the fruit) into a mixing bowl. This is the dry mixture. Combine the wet and dry ingredients and mix gently with a silicone spatula until just combined. Add 100 g/⅔ cup of the blueberries and incorporate. Do not overmix.

Oil the muffin moulds or line them with non-stick paper liners. Divide the mixture among the muffin cups. Top each muffin with a couple of the remaining 50 g/⅓ cup blueberries. Bake in the preheated oven for about 25 minutes. Allow to cool in the muffin pan for a few minutes, the transfer to a wire rack to cool completely.

These muffins are great for breakfast but also as an afternoon snack with a cup of your favourite tea blend.

3 tablespoons virgin coconut oil or extra virgin olive oil

1 very ripe banana

225 g/¾ cup rice syrup or maple syrup

420 ml/1¾ cups Milk Kefir (see pages 22–23), at room temperature (it's fine to use store-bought kefir, if necessary)

¼ teaspoon bourbon vanilla powder

130 g/1 cup unbleached plain/all-purpose flour

130 g/1 cup coconut flour

70 g ½ cup wholegrain/whole-wheat flour

¼ teaspoon salt

1 teaspoon aluminium-free baking powder

1 teaspoon bicarbonate of/baking soda

150 g/1 cup fresh blueberries or other fruit

12-hole/cup muffin pan

Makes 12

# Healing miso soup

If you've never had soup for breakfast, you should try treating yourself with a bowl of hot miso soup like this one. In Japan, miso soup is traditionally served for breakfast, accompanied by rice and pickled vegetables. It's very clear why the Japanese have the world's longest life expectancy! Apart from nourishing you with enzymes, vitamins and minerals, this delicious, energizing soup will also support your immune system – perfect if you're suffering from fatigue or the common cold. Don't forget that you can combine different kinds of miso in the same soup! Since hatcho (soy) miso is of high quality but has a strong taste, try to combine ½ tablespoon of soy miso with ½ tablespoon barley miso to get all the benefits of both kinds of soy paste. In warmer weather, you may want to substitute darker miso pastes with the milder sweet white miso.

Soak the wakame in a bowl with 120 ml/½ cup cold water until soft. Drain (reserve the water), cut into small pieces and set aside. Peel the fresh ginger and finely mince half of it. Finely grate the other half in a small bowl and keep for later. Chop the spring onions/scallions and cut the tofu into small cubes.

In a frying pan/skillet, sauté the white part of the spring onions/scallions for 1 minute in the sesame oil, then add the garlic, ginger and salt. Sauté a little longer, add the hot water, tofu and set-aside wakame and cover. Bring to the boil, then lower the heat and simmer for 4 minutes. Remove from the heat.

Pour approximately 60 ml/¼ cup of hot water into a small bowl. Add the miso and purée really well with a fork, until completely dissolved. Pour back, cover and let sit for 2–3 minutes. Take the grated ginger in your hand and squeeze it to release the juice directly into the hot soup. Discard the remaining ginger pulp. Add the chopped spring onion/scallion greens, parsley and lemon juice and serve immediately!

7-cm/3-inch piece dried wakame (seaweed)

2-cm/1-inch piece fresh ginger

4 spring onions/scallions

110 g/⅔ cup fresh tofu

2 tablespoons sesame oil

4 garlic cloves, crushed

pinch of salt

480 ml/2 cups hot water

**1–2 tablespoons barley or rice miso**

2 tablespoons fresh flat-leaf parsley, chopped

freshly squeezed juice of ½ organic lemon

Serves 2

# chapter three
# Lunch & Dinner

# Probiotic gazpacho

Gazpacho is a cold, refreshing soup, and a juicy version of a ripe summer salad. I like to add a little kefir to it and use sourdough bread instead of regular bread, which makes this gazpacho ultra-healthy. Mediterranean summers can be really hot and there are many times when this dish is the only food I feel like eating during the day!

Cut the bread into bite-sized chunks and soak in little warm water until soft. Drain and set aside.

Cut the tomatoes in half lengthwise. Use an apple grater to grate them and discard the remaining skins.

Use a pestle and mortar to pound the diced vegetables and the grated tomato, adding the pressed garlic, oil, vinegar, salt, ground pepper and the bread. Add the chilled kefir at the end to reach the desired consistency. Chill well and garnish with finely chopped basil or parsley right before serving, leaving a few leaves intact for decoration.

A pestle and mortar is traditionally used for making gazpacho, but the ingredients can also be blended before chilling, for a thick and smooth soup. However, bear in mind that the colour of the blended soup isn't as appealing as when it is pounded by hand.

100 g/3½ oz. or 1 thick slice sourdough bread (see pages 36–37 if you want to make your own sourdough bread)

3 big, ripe and juicy tomatoes (around 480 g/1 lb. total weight)

1 big cucumber, peeled and diced (around 280 g/7 oz. weight)

1 yellow (bell) pepper e.g. Babura or other sweet (bell) pepper, diced

1 small onion, finely diced

2 garlic cloves, crushed

4 tablespoons olive oil

red wine vinegar, to taste

salt, to taste

freshly ground green or black pepper

120 ml/½ cup Milk Kefir (see pages 22–23), chilled

handful of fresh basil or fresh flat-leaf parsley

Serves 4

# Hearty one-pot miso soup

Sometimes, a big bowl of this soup is the only thing I eat for lunch, especially when I feel tired and my energy is low. It's also a great late-night dinner option because it nourishes you but doesn't put too much strain on the already sleepy digestive system! Also, dried shiitake mushrooms have a relaxing effect on the body.

In a large saucepan, boil the pasta in 1.2 litres/5 cups of salted water until al dente. Strain, reserving the cooking water. Run the pasta through running cold water, drain, put in a bowl and sprinkle with the tamari and ½ tablespoon of dark sesame oil. Mix well and set aside.

In a small bowl, cover the shiitake and wakame, if using, with hot water and let soak.

Rinse the saucepan in which you cooked the pasta and add the remaining dark sesame oil. Over a medium heat sauté the garlic and ginger for 2–3 minutes, then add the onions, carrots, pumpkin cubes and a pinch of salt, mix well and sauté for 2–3 minutes. Add the turmeric, pepper and chilli powder and stir. Once the spices and vegetables start sizzling, add the reserved cooking water and another 500 ml/2 cups of hot water. Cover and bring to the boil over a medium heat. Meanwhile, drain the shiitake and wakame and chop finely, discarding the mushroom stems.

Once the soup has started to boil, add the mung beans, shiitake and wakame, lower the heat and cook, covered, for 10 minutes. Put the miso in a small bowl and pour over a ladle of hot soup. Dilute completely with the help of a small whisk or fork. Remove the soup from the heat and add the diluted miso and chopped spinach. Taste and adjust seasoning, if needed. Stir, cover and allow to rest for 1 minute.

Divide the cooked pasta among bowls and pour over the soup, making sure that each portion gets a lot of veggies and sprouts. Serve hot!

100 g/3½ oz. dried soba noodles or tagliatelle

1 teaspoon salt

½ tablespoon tamari

2½ tablespoons dark sesame oil

3 dried shiitake mushrooms

1 strip wakame seaweed (optional)

1 tablespoon chopped garlic

2 tablespoons chopped fresh ginger

1 small onion, diced

2 carrots, diced (around 100 g/ 3½ oz. total weight)

120 g/1 generous cup cubed pumpkin

¼ teaspoon ground turmeric

freshly ground black pepper

pinch of chilli powder

100 g/1½ cups mung bean sprouts

2 tablespoons rice or barley miso

130 g/4½ oz. spinach leaves, chopped

Serves 3

# Vegan BLT sandwich

If you never thought you could make a delish and healthy BLT sandwich, think again! In this recipe tempeh is transformed into crispy vegan bacon, sourdough bread is toasted just right and instead of fatty mayonnaise I'm using the tasty vegan mayonnaise dressing!

Preheat the grill/broiler to medium-high. Line a baking sheet with kitchen foil.

Cut the tempeh into the thinnest possible slices. Depending on the shape of the tempeh, you should get 20–26 slices.

In a bowl, whisk together all of the other ingredients thoroughly to make a smooth marinade.

Place the slices of tempeh on the prepared baking sheet. Cover each slice with a small amount of the marinade, spreading it to cover the entire slice. Turn them over and do the same on the other side.

Place the baking sheet in the upper part of the preheated oven. Bake for 8–10 minutes, checking occasionally as some ovens have a high grill/broiler heat and the slices could be done faster. Turn the tempeh slices and continue grilling/broiling until the marinade has soaked in and the slices are crispy and golden brown. Allow the tempeh slices to cool before making sandwiches. You can bake the tempeh a day in advance.

Toast the bread slices. To make a sandwich, spread 2 tablespoons of dressing on the bottom slice, cover with lettuce, put 5 slices of tempeh bacon on top, add 2 slices of tomato and 1 tablespoon of your chosen fermented vegetables. Top with another toasted slice of bread. Cut across to make 2 triangular sandwiches and you have a very delicious brunch, lunch or dinner!

**For the tempeh bacon:**
200 g/6½ oz. tempeh
**2 tablespoons soy sauce**
½ teaspoon sweet paprika
1 teaspoon Dijon mustard
1 teaspoon barbecue spice mix
¼ teaspoon chilli powder
2 tablespoons toasted sesame oil
½ teaspoon garlic powder
¼ teaspoon crushed black pepper

**For the sandwiches:**
**8 slices sourdough or sprouted bread (see pages 36–37 if you want to make your own sourdough bread)**
8 large leaves of Cos/Romaine lettuce, or other greens
12 large tomato slices, deseeded
½ cup Cashew Mayonnaise Dressing (see pages 116–117)
**4 tablespoons fermented vegetables: Sauerkraut with Quinces (see pages 76–77), Turshiya (see pages 72–73) or Turmeric & Chilli Kimchi, (see pages 112–113)**

Serves 4

# Beet & quinoa bowl

This simple, bright-pink dish is ideal as a light summer lunch and is a good candidate for your lunchbox. Once the beets have slightly fermented and you have added all other ingredients, it can sit in the fridge for 2 days, so it's OK to make it in advance! The flavours will develop and it will be even more delicious!

2 medium beetroot/beets,
    weighing around 400 g/14 oz.

¼ teaspoon salt

170 g/1 cup quinoa

480 ml/2 cups water

70 g/½ cup sunflower seeds
    (shelled)

**1 tablespoon umeboshi vinegar**

1 small onion

4 tablespoons chopped fresh
    flat-leaf parsley

4 tablespoons olive oil

freshly squeezed lemon juice or
    apple cider vinegar, to taste

salt and crushed black pepper,
    to taste

pickle press (optional)

1-litre/quart preserving jar

Serves 4

Wash, peel and finely grate the beetroot/beets. Put in a bowl, add the salt and squeeze really well with your hands until the beetroot/beet flesh starts 'sweating'. Cover with a small plate that fits into the bowl, top with something heavy and allow to rest for 24 hours. If you have a small pickle press, use this instead. If there isn't enough juice to cover the beetroot/beets, add just enough salted water to cover. Before using the beetroot/beets in this salad, drain off most of the pickle juice.

Put the quinoa in a sieve/strainer and rinse well under running water. Drain. Put the drained quinoa into the preserving jar covered with 480 ml/2 cups water. Loosely cover the jar with a lid or with muslin/cheesecloth with a rubber band tied around it. Let the quinoa soak for 24 hours at room temperature.

Put both the quinoa and the soaking water in a saucepan, bring to a boil, add a few pinches of salt, lower the heat to its minimum setting, half-cover the saucepan and cook until the quinoa absorbs all the water, about 15 minutes. Remove from the heat and allow to cool. Meanwhile, rinse the sunflower seeds under running water and drain well. Put the seeds in a frying pan/skillet over a medium heat and dry-roast, stirring vigorously until the seeds start sizzling and turn golden brown. Pour into a clean bowl and, while still hot, pour over 1 tablespoon of umeboshi vinegar and stir until absorbed. If you don't have umeboshi vinegar, dissolve ¼ teaspoon of salt in ½ tablespoon hot water and pour over the seeds. Stir until absorbed.

Finely chop the onion and the parsley. In a large glass mixing bowl, gently mix all the ingredients and season with olive oil, lemon juice or cider vinegar and salt and pepper. Garnish with more chopped parsley. Refrigerate shortly before serving. This salad is rich in essential amino acids and good fats from the seeds. It's also full of minerals from the beetroot/beets, parsley and onions, so enjoy every mouthful!

# Vegan Greek salad with tofu feta

The key to this beautiful Greek salad is the blend of bold flavours from fresh seasonal vegetables, high-quality olives and olive oil, and creamy fermented tofu. Make sure you use organic ingredients since they taste so much better and you won't need to peel the cucumber.

Slice the block of tofu lengthwise into four equally thick slices. Spread 75 g/⅓ cup of miso over each slice, covering it entirely. Place the tofu slices in a glass container. Cover and let sit at room temperature for 24 hours. The tofu will absorb the saltiness and taste of the miso paste. Scrape off the miso (save it to make soup) and rinse quickly under running water, if necessary. and that's all there is to it!

I often ferment tofu in advance and pack it in jars, covered in olive oil, adding Mediterranean herbs, garlic, olives, dried tomatoes and chilli for an extra flavour . I'll use it throughout that month to make vegan Greek salad, or serve it as an appetizer.

Cut the 2 tomatoes and (bell) pepper into large rounds. Cut the cucumber, with the skin on, in half lengthwise and slice into wedges. Cut the cherry tomatoes in half, and chop the onion into thin half-moons. Roughly chop the basil, leaving a couple of leaves whole, for decoration. Put all the vegetables into a large salad bowl, add the olives, basil, dried herbs, olive oil, a pinch of salt, crushed black pepper and vinegar, to taste. Quickly toss the ingredients together, preferably with your hands.

To serve, divide among 4 small plates or shallow bowls, top with the fermented tofu cubes, and finish with a sprinkling of dried herbs and a drizzling of olive oil. Garnish with whole basil leaves and enjoy immediately!

**For fermenting the tofu:**

4 slices plain, extra-firm tofu, (around 440 g/14 oz. total weight)

300 g /1¼ cups barley or rice miso

**For the salad:**

2 ripe tomatoes (around 340 g/ 12 oz. total weight)

1 green (bell) pepper, washed and deseeded

1 medium cucumber (around 200 g/7 oz. total weight)

100 g/⅔ cup ripe cherry tomatoes

1 medium red onion, peeled

20 g/½ cup fresh basil leaves

90 g/½ cup oven-dried black olives, stoned/pitted

1 teaspoon dried Mediterranean herbs

4 tablespoons extra virgin olive oil

sea salt and crushed black pepper, to taste

apple cider vinegar, to taste

Serves 4

# Koshari (Egyptian lentil & rice stew)

I first heard of koshari as a filling vegan side dish, and after testing many different versions of it, I ended up making my own Egyptian-inspired stew that is both tasty and filling, too. Lentils and rice are cooked together to cut down on the cooking stages, and I ferment the rice and soak the lentils to make this delicious dish easier to digest.

50 g/¼ cup short-grain brown rice

50 g/¼ cup sweet brown rice

**2 tablespoons yogurt whey or kefir whey (see pages 22–23)**

100 g/½ cup green or brown lentils

small piece of kombu seaweed (optional)

2 dried bay leaves

100 ml/scant ½ cup olive oil

240 g/2 full cups onion, cut into thin half-moons

½ teaspoon salt

110 g/1 full cup carrots, cut into matchsticks

¼ teaspoon ground cinnamon

⅛ teaspoon chilli powder

¾ teaspoon cumin seeds, crushed

4 whole cloves

3 tablespoons soy sauce

1 tablespoon apple cider vinegar

3 tablespoons flat-leaf parsley, chopped

2 tablespoons tomato sauce (optional)

720-ml/24 fl. oz. preserving jar

Serves 3

Mix both rices together, wash, drain, put in a clean glass jar and cover with 240 ml/1 cup of water. Add the whey, stir and cover with muslin/cheesecloth or a paper towel. Let the mixture ferment at room temperature for at least 24 hours, but ideally 2–3 days (if fermenting for over 24 hours in the summer, put the mixture in the fridge, though). Discard the soaking water.

Wash the lentils and soak them at room temperature for 24 hours in the preserving jar covered with 480 ml/2 cups water. Loosely cover the jar with a lid or with muslin/cheesecloth with a rubber band tied around it. Discard the water.

Combine the soaked rice, lentils and reserved lentil soaking water in a saucepan. Pour over 1.2 litres/5 cups of water, add the kombu (if using) and the bay leaves. Bring to the boil, lower the heat and cover. Cook for 35–40 minutes. There should be enough water to make a thick stew. If it's too thick, add a little more hot water while cooking.

Meanwhile, prepare the vegetables. Heat the oil in a frying pan/skillet, add the onions and ¼ teaspoon of salt and mix well over a medium heat. Add the carrots and another ¼ teaspoon of salt and mix again. Lower the heat to its minimum setting and sauté for 10 minutes, covered. Add the cinnamon, chilli powder, crushed cumin seeds and cloves, stir well and continue to sauté for another 15 minutes, until completely soft, creamy and slightly caramelized. Pour in the soy sauce and vinegar, stir and sauté for another 2 minutes.

When the rice and lentils are soft and creamy, add ⅔ of the sautéed vegetables to the saucepan containing the lentils and mix well to get a thick stew. Taste and adjust the seasoning if necessary and add the chopped parsley. Serve in bowls or soup plates, add a couple of tablespoons of tomato sauce (if using) on top of each serving and divide the leftover sautéed vegetables among the portions. Enjoy with a slice of sourdough or kefir bread and a bowl of greens!

# Yota (Istrian stew)

Yota is a typical Istrian stew, also popular in some parts of Slovenia and northern Italy. The main ingredients are borlotti beans and sauerkraut, which makes this a strong and filling winter dish. Another ingredient that is never omitted by Istrian *nonnas* is spare ribs, so in case you want to get the authentic smell and taste of yota, make sure you add them. For vegan yota, a piece of smoked tofu/seitan can be added instead, but only at the end of cooking. I avoid adding all the sauerkraut at once, but leave a third of the amount to add when the stew is ready, in order to benefit from live cultures in the sauerkraut that are deactivated with cooking.

Soak the beans in 2.4 litres/10 cups of water for 24 hours. Bring the beans to the boil in the soaking water, and then discard the water. Put the drained beans, bay leaves, chilli, kombu, spare ribs (if using) and 1.7 litres/7 cups of water in the pressure cooker. Securely close the lid, put on high heat and wait for the pressure to rise. Lower the heat to a minimum and cook for 45 minutes. If you are not using a pressure cooker, cook in a saucepan with a matching lid, covered, until the beans get soft, adding a little extra water during cooking, if necessary.

Meanwhile, peel and cut potatoes into quarters. If you are using tofu/seitan instead of spare ribs, cut into small cubes.

If using a pressure cooker, wait for the pressure to come down, and open the lid. Remove the bay leaves, take out the kombu (if using), chop it and put it back into the pot. Add the potatoes, 200 g/1 cup of the sauerkraut and smoked tofu/seitan (if using) and cook covered (not under pressure) for 20 minutes. Take out the potatoes and press them through a potato ricer or mash them with a fork. Return to the pot. Add sweet paprika, freshly ground black pepper, the vegetable stock cube and salt and bring to the boil. Turn off the heat and add the remaining 100 g/½ cup of sauerkraut, crushed garlic and olive oil. Taste and adjust the seasoning if necessary. The stew should be creamy and thick. If too dense, add a little more hot water. Ideally, yota should sit covered for at least 30 minutes before serving, but if you're in a hurry you can serve it immediately. Leftovers are very tasty the next day, or even the second day after cooking.

340 g/2 cups dried borlotti beans

3 dried bay leaves

1 small dried chilli

1 strip kombu seaweed (optional)

200 g/6½ oz. spare ribs or smoked tofu/seitan

2 small potatoes (around 210 g/ 7½ oz. total weight)

300 g/1½ cups Sauerkraut with Quinces (see pages 76–77)

2 garlic cloves, crushed

2 tablespoons olive oil

1 teaspoon sweet paprika

½ teaspoon sea salt

1 vegetable stock/bouilllon cube

freshly ground black pepper

pressure cooker (optional)

Serves 4

# Fettucine Alfredo

My favourite pasta dishes are the most simple ones: pasta with garlic and olive oil or the famous Fettuccine Alfredo, which I'm sharing here. The original recipe calls for a lot of butter and Parmigiano Reggiano cheese, but I am not a fan of butter and large quantities of aged cheese, so my version consists of freshly made fettuccine, home-made cream cheese and a drizzle of olive oil. It's a very simple and comforting dish.

300 g/4½ cups fresh thin
  fettuccine, or 200 g/7 oz.
  dry fettuccine

4–6 tablespoons olive oil

360 ml/1½ cups Yogurt Cream
  Cheese or Kefir Cream Cheese
  (see pages 18–19)

freshly ground sea salt

freshly ground black pepper

2 tablespoons freshly chopped
  flat-leaf parsley or other fresh
  herbs (optional)

Serves 2

Add the pasta to a large pot of salted boiling water. If using fresh fettuccine cook for 2–3 minutes until al dente (neither hard nor soft). Dry pasta needs to cook for longer so check the instructions on the package. Drain and reserve 4 tablespoons of the cooking water, to serve.

Place the pasta in a serving bowl. Add the reserved cooking water, olive oil and cream cheese and season with salt and pepper. Toss gently until well combined. Adjust seasoning to taste (remember that the pasta was cooked in salted water).

Serve immediately. You may want to drizzle some more olive oil at this point. Sprinkling some chopped fresh flat-leaf parsley or other fresh herbs add colour and flavour, but this dish really is a celebration of simplicity and deliciousness and garnishes are optional.

chapter four
# Side salads & snacks

# Turshiya (mixed vegetables in brine)

Many different types of fermenting and pickling can be found under the name *turshiya* throughout the Balkans and the Middle East but not all are the result of natural fermentation. However, the healthiest way to make it is to simply immerse big chunks of vegetables into a brine (containing 4–5% salt) and let the good bacteria and yeasts work with the enzymes of the vegetables!

Wash the vegetables (do not scrub them too hard, though, because this removes enzymes beneficial for fermentation) and remove any dark spots. Remove any leaves from the cauliflower and break it into fairly large florets. Leave the carrots whole or slice them lengthwise. Peel the onions and cut into quarters. Slice the peppers in half lengthwise, remove the stem and seeds and cut each half again lengthwise into 2–3 slices. Cut the cucumbers into thick half-moons, with the skin on. Place all the vegetables into the crock or bucket. In a separate bowl, whisk together the water and salt until dissolved. Pour over the vegetables.

Find a plate or lid that fits into the crock or bucket and place over the vegetables to keep them submerged in the brine at all times. Use a small stone to keep the lid from floating, if necessary. It is not necessary to create pressure to make turshiya. Cover with a clean tea/dish towel and let sit at room temperature, but away from direct sunlight. The fermentation process will start in about 2 days with some foam forming on the surface of the liquid. Check the crock or bucket every 2–3 days, remove any mould that might appear and continue fermenting. Depending on the room temperature the vegetables can be ready in 3–4 weeks, but in colder temperatures it can take up to 2 months. Be patient, check your crock or bucket frequently and taste the vegetables from time to time to see how the flavour is developing. After they are sour to your taste, pack them in clean jars, cover in the brine and keep refrigerated.

Turshiya can last for a long time, but because vegetables fermented this way are so tasty and can be eaten with every meal, I never had it refrigerated for too long! Plan ahead and ferment a new batch while you're eating the one you have just prepared. To really exploit the potential of fermented foods, it is best to keep a small quantity at room temperature 2–3 hours before serving, since the good bacteria are more or less dormant in the fridge.

Serve a tablespoon of fermented vegetables at every meal for better digestion.

1 small cauliflower (around 480 g/ 17 oz. in weight)

8 small carrots (around 220 g/8 oz. total weight)

4 small onions (around 320 g/11½ oz. total weight)

4 green Babura peppers or other sweet (bell) peppers (around 400 g/14 oz. total weight)

2 cucumbers (around 450 g/16 oz. total weight)

3 litres/quarts water

120 g/½ cup sea salt

3-litre/quart pickle press

7-litre/7½-quart crock, bucket or similar

Makes 1 x 7-litre/7½-quart jar, crock or bucket

# Cultured salsa cruda

This is a wonderful way to ferment late spring and summer vegetables and fruits and use up any spare yogurt/kefir whey. Brine would be enough as a fermenting medium, but whey speeds up the process slightly and adds extra enzymes, so why not? Ripe fruit gives a nice sweet kick to this salsa. Instead of cherries you could use a ripe mango, apricot, peach or plum.

1 cucumber (around 220 g/7¾ oz. in weight)

2 ripe tomatoes (around 340 g/ 12 oz. total weight)

2 onions (around 140 g/5 oz. total weight)

25 g/½ cup sliced spring onion/scallion greens, chopped parsley or dill

freshly squeezed juice of 1 lemon

1 mild fresh chilli/chile pepper

70 g/½ cup ripe cherries, stoned/pitted

20 g/1 generous tablespoon Himalayan pink salt (fine grain), or other salt

960 g/4 cups yogurt whey or kefir whey (see pages 22–23) or water

2-litre/quart glass jar with tightly fitting lid

Makes 1 x 2-litre/quart jar

Peel the cucumber if it hasn't been organically grown. Chop all the vegetables and put in a big bowl. Add the lemon juice, sliced chilli/chile pepper and the cherries. Whisk the salt and yogurt whey or kefir whey together well in the jar, then add the bowl contents and mix well. Close tightly and let sit at room temperature for up to 10 days – in summer it will be ready after around 4 days.

Open the lid a couple of times during the day because carbon dioxide, which is the by-product of fermentation, builds up inside the jar. Alternatively, seal the jar with muslin/cheesecloth and string; however, the end product will be less fizzy. When the vegetables are sour to your taste, keep them in the fridge and eat up the salsa within a month. A spoonful or two of cultured salsa cruda is a great condiment with any meal and can also be added to your everyday salad. It's very refreshing!

# Sauerkraut with quinces

Sauerkraut is definitely one of the winter staple foods in both my family and most of the families I know, and we all grew up participating in the ritual of preparing sauerkraut from an early age as kids. I remember my cousins and I being asked to jump on top of the cabbage to pack it tightly into the barrel! The quinces add a nice yellow hue to the entire batch and my in-laws always add them into the huge barrel of cabbage that bubbles away in their kitchen every winter. Some people add apples instead of quinces, which can be difficult to find. Nowadays, I'm never out of sauerkraut – one batch is always in use while another one is fermenting!

3 medium cabbage heads (around 2.4 kg/5 lbs. total weight)
60 g/3 tablespoons sea salt
2 quinces or apples
1 tablespoon whole black peppercorns
10 dried bay leaves
3-litre/quart pickle press, crock or bucket

Makes 1 x 3-litre/quart jar or 2 x smaller jars

Wash the cabbage well. Slice in half and remove the hearts. Grate finely using a cabbage grater, or chop as finely as you can with a sharp vegetable knife. Put the chopped cabbage in a large bowl and sprinkle with the salt. Start squeezing the cabbage with your clean hands – the salt will pull the water out of the cabbage and create enough juice to serve as the brine in which the cabbage will be submerged during fermentation. Core and slice the quinces or apples and add to the salted cabbage. Mix well and add the peppercorns and bay leaves.

Pack into the pickle press, then screw down the lid until the juice covers the cabbage completely. Or, if using a crock or bucket, cover with a plate that fits inside, press it down and place some kind of weight on top of the plate (it can be a 1 kg/2¼-lb. weight, a clean stone or a big jar filled with water and closed tightly). Make sure that the cabbage is submerged in the brine for the entire time during fermentation. If you used late autumn/fall cabbage, it might not be very juicy and there won't be enough liquid to cover. If that is the case, add enough salted water to keep the cabbage under the liquid (25 g/2 tablespoons of salt per 1 litre/quart of water). Cover the pickle press, crock or bucket with a large tea/dish towel to protect from the cabbage from flies and dust. Leave to ferment for 4 weeks (or longer in winter) at room temperature, checking it from time to time and removing any mould from the surface of the brine. After 4 weeks, the sauerkraut should be crunchy, sour and very tasty. At this point, I pack it in glass jars with the brine and keep it in the fridge.

# Purple sauerkraut with dulse & caraway seeds

We should always have a rainbow of colours on our plates, and this red cabbage fermented into a purple kraut will brighten up any meal! To boost the mineral intake I often add seaweed to my fermentation crocks, and spices are also a welcome addition; caraway seeds in this sauerkraut make it very aromatic. Try this combination – you won't be disappointed!

1½ teaspoons caraway seeds

10 g/½ oz. dulse seaweed

1 medium head red cabbage, (around 800 g/28 oz. in weight)

2½ teaspoons salt

pickle press, clean glass jar or crock

Makes 200 g/2 cups

Use a pestle and mortar to crush the caraway seeds. Cover the dulse with water and let it soak for 10 minutes. Very finely chop or grate the cabbage. Add the salt and squeeze with clean hands – this will help to release the juices. Add the drained and chopped seaweed and crushed caraway seeds.

The cabbage should be dripping wet. To ensure proper fermentation without the presence of oxygen, carefully pack the spiced cabbage with its juice in a pickle press, a big jar or a crock. It should always be submerged in its own brine, so stuff it tightly and screw down the lid of the pickle press as much as you can, or if using a jar or crock, pack tightly, cover with a plate that fits inside and place some kind of weight on top (like a glass bottle filled with water, a marble weight or a stone).

Check after 12 hours and press again; the cabbage will wilt further and more juice will come out. The shortest fermentation time for the process to start is 3 days, but I usually leave it for at least 7 days and ideally for 4 weeks. During the fermentation, it's necessary to check your press, jar or crock every other day and remove any foam and/or mould that might form on the surface of the brine – a common and normal event that will not, in any way, affect the quality of your sauerkraut.

After 4 weeks transfer the sauerkraut to jars, cover in brine and refrigerate. It will stay fresh for at least 1 month and possibly 2–3 months. Bring to room temperature before eating to ensure that you're taking in the maximum amount of good bacteria. Enjoy!

# Quick radish tsukemono

This is the simplest and quickest method to transform many types of vegetables from raw and hard to soft, juicy and easy to digest. The fermentation starts once the salt from the soy sauce penetrates the vegetables and they start sweating, and it takes from 1–2 hours for this type of salad to be ready for serving, depending on the type of vegetable – much shorter than the usual 4 weeks needed for fermentation! Daikon radish/mooli is a typical ingredient used to make a traditional Japanese tsukemono, but I use the local radish variety: red radish in spring and summer and black radish in autumn/fall and winter. Radishes are well known for their detoxification properties and are a great help with digesting fatty foods, so be sure to have this tsukemono to hand when serving fried foods.

500 g/1 lb. 2 oz. red or black radishes

rind of 1 organic lemon

3-cm/1¼-inch kombu strip, thinly shredded (optional)

**4 tablespoons soy sauce or tamari**

pickle press, clean glass jar or crock

Makes 1 x 720-ml/24-fl. oz. jar

If using red radishes, wash and slice them into 0.5-cm/³⁄₁₆-inch thick rounds. You can also finely chop their greens and ferment them together. If using black radish, wash and cut each radish into wedges. Slice into 0.5-cm/³⁄₁₆-inch thick pieces.

Pat dry the radish pieces with a tea/dish towel or a paper towel. In a bowl, combine the soy sauce or tamari, lemon rind and kombu seaweed, then add the radish slices and squeeze well with clean hands so that the radish absorbs the marinade and starts sweating. Place in a pickle press and screw down the lid as tightly as you can. Screw the lid down every 15 minutes or so. After 1–2 hours, the radishes should have released enough water to cover. Mix well and serve as a side condiment or a small salad. It will keep in a jar in the fridge for a couple of days.

# Scandinavian chanterelle salad

Wild mushrooms are very nutritious, and when in season, numerous types of wild mushrooms can be found in farmers' markets around the world. Chanterelles are one of my favourites; they have a sweet, peach-like scent and their mild flavour combines well with many different ingredients. I tried a dish similar to this one while travelling through Denmark, but I prefer substituting the double/heavy cream with my home-fermented yogurt/kefir cheese (see pages 26–27), which makes this salad very light. It also works really well as a sandwich dressing, too. Feel free to use other mushrooms if chanterelles aren't available.

Gently wipe the chanterelles to remove any dirt. Do not wash them if not absolutely necessary, but if they are really dirty, quickly rinse them and pat dry immediately with a paper towel. Slice the mushrooms and put them in a bowl. Add the onion, lemon juice, tamari or soy sauce, agave syrup and salt and pepper. Mix well so that the marinade coats all mushroom pieces. Cover and let marinate for 1 hour at room temperature, or longer if refrigerated.

Mix in the chilled cream cheese and adjust the seasoning. Serve immediately, since the mushrooms continue releasing their juices and the salad might become watery.

140 g/2½ cups fresh chanterelle mushrooms

2 tablespoons finely chopped onion

freshly squeezed juice of ½ organic lemon

2 teaspoon tamari or soy sauce

1 teaspoon agave syrup

¼ teaspoon salt

freshly ground black pepper

240 ml/1 cup Yogurt Cream Cheese or Kefir Cream Cheese (see pages 26–27)

Serves 2

# Tender spring rolls with fermented onion

The choice of fillings for spring rolls is endless; you can actually fill them with any leftovers and make a fancy lunch in no time! Even though raw fillings can be nice and refreshing, I prefer sautéing vegetables in a wok for a couple of minutes. Any vegetables will do. Fermented onion slices are an excellent addition. They will add crunchiness, taste and, of course, extra enzymes.

1 medium courgette/zucchini (around 200 g/7 oz. in weight)

2 small carrots (around 100 g/ 3½ oz. total weight)

1 small onion

45 ml/3 tablespoons olive oil

pinch of sea salt

140 g/1 cup fresh peas (or frozen)

150 g/2 cups shredded cabbage

½ teaspoon Himalayan pink salt or other coarse-grain salt

¼ teaspoon ground turmeric

**1 tablespoon soy sauce or tamari**

14 round rice paper wrappers, 22 cm/9 inches in diameter

85 g/3 oz. Onion Anchovies (see pages 110–111)

Makes 14 rolls

Cut the courgette/zucchini and carrots into julienne strips and slice the onions into thin half-moons. Heat a wok (preferably cast-iron) and add the oil, onions and a pinch of sea salt. Stir constantly over a medium heat to coat the onions in oil. Add the carrots, peas and cabbage and ¼ teaspoon of Himalayan pink salt (or other coarse-grain salt) and continue stirring until the peas are soft enough, for about 6–10 minutes. Add the courgette/zucchini, the remaining ¼ teaspoon of Himalayan pink salt (or other coarse-grain salt) and turmeric, and stir for another minute. Add the soy sauce or tamari and combine well. Remove from the heat.

Half-fill a large soup bowl with warm water – the rice paper should fit inside it. Spread a clean cotton tea/dish towel on a work surface. Quickly immerse 1 rice paper at a time in the water. Do not soak it, otherwise it will either break or get sticky and unusable. It should remain slightly firm and should not fold in on itself. Place it carefully on the upper part of the tea/dish towel. Fold the bottom of the towel over it and pat dry.

Starting from the ⅓ of rice paper closest to you, place 2 tablespoons of the filling and cover with 2 slices of fermented onion. First gently pull away the left edge of the wrapper from the tea/dish towel over the filling, then fold over the bottom edge and start rolling, tucking the filling with the help of your forefingers, so that the roll remains compact. When done with rolling, pick up the roll, which should still have the right side open and rice paper hanging, and tuck in the extra paper, closing the spring roll. If you're not going to serve them right away, place them on a tray without touching each other, cover with clingfilm/plastic wrap and store at room temperature for a couple of hours. If you are going to use them as an on-the-move snack, wrap each roll individually in clingfilm/plastic wrap. This way they will remain fresh and won't stick together. Bon appétit!

# Temaki rolls with fermented seed pâté

This hand-rolled sushi is really easy to make. Temakis are a great choice for sushi parties since they are best rolled directly at the table, just before eating, and everybody can join in, which leaves you with less work! Prepare and serve all ingredients in the middle of the table and let the fun begin!

First make the pâté. Soak the pumpkin seeds in 840 ml/3½ cups of water (preferably non-chlorinated) for 2–3 days, until slightly fermented, without changing the soaking water. Discard the soaking water and rinse them thoroughly under running water. Drain well. Place in a high-speed blender jug/pitcher, together with the remaining ingredients. Blend until smooth, using a tamper tool to push down the ingredients. If you don't own a high-speed blender, the pâté will probably turn out chunkier in a less powerful blender, and more water will need to be added, resulting in a somewhat runnier consistency. Do not halve this recipe, since the blender needs the amount of at least 2 cups in order to make a smooth paste. Let sit in the fridge for another day; the flavours really develop in this final stage of setting. There will be some leftovers, but you can easily store this pâté in the fridge and use it as a dip or as a spread within a week.

Wash and julienne the carrots. Peel the avocado, slice in half, discard the stone and cut both halves in strips. Wash the rocket/arugula or sprouts and pat dry. Take only the green parts of the spring onions/scallions, wash them well and cut into 10-cm/4-inch pieces. Cut each nori sheet in half with scissors.

Make sure your hands are dry before starting. Place a piece of nori (shiny side down) in the palm of your hand and add 1½ tablespoons of pumpkin seed pâté. Spread it gently on the left third of the nori sheet. Place your chosen fillings diagonally over the pate. Do not overfill; a couple of carrot matchsticks, 1 slice of avocado, 1 tablespoon of sauerkraut and some greens are more than enough. Fold the bottom left corner of the nori over and begin rolling into a cone shape. Wet the edge with little water and seal. Continue until all nori is used. Serve the temaki rolls with more fermented vegetables, condiments, some soy sauce and leftover greens. They are the healthiest snack out there!

**For the pâté:**

240 g/2 cups pumpkin seeds

840 ml/3½ cups water, for soaking

50 ml/scant ¼ cup olive oil

60 ml/¼ cup water

1 garlic clove

¼ teaspoon turmeric powder

1 tablespoon nutritional yeast (optional)

3 teaspoons rice or barley miso

2 teaspoons lemon juice

¼ teaspoon salt

freshly crushed black pepper

Makes 250 g/2½ cups

**For the rolls:**

6 sheets of nori seaweed

2 medium carrots (around 100 g/3½ oz. total weight)

**2 cups Sauerkraut with Quinces (see pages 76–77) or other fermented vegetables**

1 ripe avocado (around 190 g/ 6½ oz. in weight)

3 spring onions/scallions

2 handfuls arugula/rocket or 50 g/1 cup alfalfa sprouts

Makes 12

# Sarma (sour cabbage rolls)

Sarma rolls are the best autumn and winter comfort food I can think of and make for a hearty snack or a main meal. Pickled whole cabbage heads are very easily found in food shops and farmers markets in south-eastern Europe, but perhaps not so easily in northern Europe and in the UK. However, Eastern food shops and markets very often carry whole cabbage heads pickled in brine. Sarma rolls are traditionally filled with minced/ground meat, but I always fill them with freshly fermented tempeh, which I buy locally. So this is a double-ferment dish, offering a combination of sauerkraut and tempeh to warm up your body and soul!

1 small pickled whole cabbage head (around 900 g/2 lbs. in weight)

100 ml/scant ½ cup olive oil

1 small onion

3 garlic cloves, crushed

50 g/½ cup finely chopped leeks

150 g/1½ cups finely chopped fresh cabbage

2 carrots, finely chopped (around 130 g/4½ oz. total weight)

½ teaspoon salt

½ vegetable stock/bouillon cube

¼ teaspoon ground turmeric

⅛ teaspoon chilli powder

½ teaspoon dried oregano leaves

**2 tablespoons tamari or soy sauce**

250 g/2½ cups tempeh, crushed with a fork

1 teaspoon sweet paprika

3 dried bay leaves

Makes 14

Turn the pickled cabbage head over, and carve out the remains of the middle stem, to release the leaves. Separate the leaves and, with the help of a paring knife, thin the tough ribs at the bottom of each leaf. Be careful not to damage the leaves. This will make it easier to roll the sarma.

Lightly heat the olive oil in a large frying pan/skillet, and add the chopped onion, garlic, leek, cabbage and carrots. Add salt, stir well, lower the heat to a minimum, cover and sauté until soft, about 20 minutes. Add the ½ stock cube, turmeric, chilli powder, oregano and tamari or soy sauce and stir well until fragrant. Add the tempeh and stir well. Sauté for another 5 minutes. Add 1–2 spoonfuls of water, if necessary.

Take a cabbage leaf, place it in your left palm, heap 4 tablespoons of the filling near the bottom of the leaf, fold the bottom side towards the centre, then the left and the right sides. Roll completely and then tuck in the top, forming a compact roll that won't fall apart during cooking. Continue this process – this amount of topping should be enough for filling 14 leaves. Finely chop the remaining sour cabbage leaves and place them on the bottom of a wider heavy-bottomed saucepan. Place all the rolls on top of the shredded cabbage, cover with 720 ml/3 cups of water, add the sweet paprika and bay leaves, cover and bring to a slow boil. Simmer for 40 minutes. Serve with polenta or mashed potatoes. Sarma can sit in the fridge for 3 days and is even better when eaten the next day. Enjoy!

chapter five

Breads &
pancakes

# Sourdough bread

This is the most traditional and natural way to bake bread and, because of the long and natural fermentation process, sourdough bread is much easier to digest than any other type of bread. I just love the smell of fermented dough when it's rising, and I love the smell of sourdough bread when it's baking even more!

In a big bowl whisk all the 'sponge' ingredients thoroughly into a thick batter. Cover with a clean, damp tea/dish towel and let sit in the oven with only the light switched on (i.e. without setting a temperature) for 8–12 hours, or until bubbly.

Add the salt to the sponge and stir well. Add the flour and stir vigorously until the dough is thick and you need to stop stirring and start kneading. Knead the bread on a clean work surface, sprinkling more flour as necessary to prevent sticking. The longer you knead, the better: continue for at least 5 minutes to develop elasticity. Oil a clean bowl, place the dough in it and oil it as well. Cover the bowl with a clean, wet tea/dish towel and allow to sit in the oven with only the light switched on again. The dough is ready when it has increased in size by about 50 per cent, which can be between 8–24 hours.

In order to get a nicely shaped loaf, cut a sheet of parchment paper to fit inside the loaf pan without any creases. Flatten the risen dough slightly (sprinkle a little more flour if necessary), shape into a loaf and transfer into the pan. Let rise in the oven for another 2 hours or so.

Preheat the oven to 220°C (425°F) Gas 8. Place the pan in the middle of the preheated oven, lower the heat to 200°C (400°F) Gas 6 and bake for 1 hour. You can take the bread out of the oven, tip it out of the pan and tap the bottom of the loaf – it should sound hollow. If not, return to the pan and into the oven for another 10 minutes.

Remove from the pan, peel off the parchment paper and let cool slightly before cutting. If you want a softer crust, wrap the warm bread in a clean, damp tea/dish towel and let cool. To store the sourdough bread, wrap it in a clean, dry tea/dish towel and place inside a paper bag. This bread does not spoil or mould easily, so it can be consumed up to 2 weeks after baking. It will harden, but can be sliced and steamed to soften up before serving.

**For the 'sponge':**

240 g/1 cup yogurt whey or kefir whey (see pages 26 27) or water

260 g/1 cup Sourdough Starter (see pages 36–37)

260 g/2 cups wheat or spelt flour

**For the bread:**

½ teaspoon salt

260 g/2 cups flour of your choice (rye, barley, wholemeal/whole wheat, etc.)

450-g/1-lb. loaf pan

Makes 1 x 450-g/1-lb. loaf

# Sourdough grissini

When I'm feeding my sourdough starter and need to discard some of the fermented starter to add fresh flour, instead of throwing the extra starter away (which would be a big shame and quite wasteful), I use it to make these grissini or sourdough crackers. This more-ish snack is virtually unspoilable; I once made a big batch and left them in a cupboard for 1 month, and apart from turning a bit soft, they were still good with no traces of mould. Now that's something!

260 g/2 cups wholemeal/
   whole-wheat flour, plus
   extra for kneading

130 g/1 cup spelt or barley flour

1½ teaspoons salt

2 tablespoons olive oil

120 ml/½ cup yogurt whey or kefir
   whey (see pages 26–27)

80 ml/⅓ cup water

230 g/1 generous cup Sourdough
   Starter (see pages 36–37)

salt, dried herbs, crushed black
   pepper and sesame seeds,
   for sprinkling

olive oil, for brushing

Makes 30 grissini (28 cm/11 inches
   long)

**For the paprika cream cheese:**

240 g/1 cup Yogurt Cream Cheese
   or Kefir Cream Cheese (see pages
   26–27)

1 teaspoon sweet paprika

¼ teaspoon salt

2 tablespoons sesame or sunflower oil

1 tablespoon finely minced onion

pinch of chilli/hot pepper flakes

Makes 250 g/1 cup

In a large bowl, whisk the flours and salt. Add the olive oil and incorporate. Add the remaining ingredients and mix with a spatula until a moist dough forms. If the bowl is large enough, knead the dough inside it, adding a little flour if necessary to produce a medium-soft dough. Continue kneading for 3–5 minutes. Oil the bowl and the top of the dough, cover with a clean, wet cloth/rag and allow to rise for at least 2 hours in a warm place. The dough must double in size. I usually make the dough a day in advance, place the covered bowl in the oven with only the oven light on, and let it rise overnight.

Preheat the oven to 180°C (350°F) Gas 4.

Line 2 baking sheets with parchment paper. Before rolling the grissini, knead the dough once more. Take 1 tablespoon of the dough at a time and roll each breadstick on a lightly floured work surface until about 28 cm/11 inches long. Gently transfer them onto the parchment-lined baking sheets. Brush each stick with little olive oil and sprinkle with your choice of topping. Bake for around 30 minutes in 2 batches, turning them halfway through cooking.

Meanwhile, make the paprika cream cheese. Mix all the ingredients together well and allow to sit at room temperature for 30 minutes before serving, so that the flavours blend together nicely.

Allow the grissini to cool and either eat or store in a resealable plastic bag. Serve with the paprika cream cheese or herbed cream cheese (see page 97).

# Sourdough crackers

This is another great way to use extra sourdough starter that would otherwise be discarded. These crackers are really crispy but be careful when baking, because one minute too long in the oven and they will get very hard after cooling.

If necessary, melt the coconut oil by placing its jar in a pot of hot water. Whisk the coconut oil or olive oil together with the sourdough starter and salt, then start adding flour, mixing constantly until the dough becomes firmer and you can start kneading it. Form into a stiff dough. Cover and let sit in a warm place for at least 7 hours.

Preheat the oven to 200°C (400°F) Gas 6.

Meanwhile, make the herbed cream cheese. Mix all the ingredients together well and let sit in the fridge for 30 minutes before serving, so that the flavours blend nicely.

Divide the dough into 2 equal parts. Use a rolling pin to spread the dough thinly over a piece of parchment paper, then repeat with the other piece of dough. With a pizza cutter or a knife, cut the crackers into desired shapes. I like smaller rectangles and can get about 45 pieces out of this dough. Prick each cracker with a fork a couple of times and transfer the crackers (on their parchment paper) to a baking sheet. Bake in 2–3 batches until lightly golden but not browned, about 12 minutes. Cool and store in a resealable plastic bag. These crackers will keep for many weeks.

60 ml/¼ cup virgin coconut oil or extra virgin olive oil

260 g/1 cup **Sourdough Starter (see pages 36–37)**

½ teaspoon salt

200 g/1½ cups wholemeal/ whole-wheat flour

olive oil and coarse sea salt

**For the herbed cream cheese:**

240 g/1 cup **Yogurt Cream Cheese or Kefir Cream Cheese (see pages 26–27)**

½ teaspoon dried oregano

½ teaspoon dried thyme

½ teaspoon dried basil

¼ teaspoon salt

2 tablespoons olive oil

1 garlic clove, crushed

crushed black pepper, to taste

Makes about 45

# Pesto focaccia

Focaccia dough has a special texture and taste due to a slightly higher oil content. It's very easy to eat too much, especially if it's still warm, with its delightfully crunchy crust and a soft inside! Apart from serving it with freshly made pesto, I often serve it with freshly prepared tomato sauce and a bowl of salad, as a summer lunch.

**For the sponge:**

200 g/¾ cup **Sourdough Starter** (see pages 36–37)

120 ml/½ cup warm water

2 tablespoons olive oil

½ tablespoon honey

70 g/½ cup rye flour

**For the dough:**

50 ml/scant ¼ cup olive oil

200 g/2½ cups flour mix (wheat, oat, rye), plus extra for kneading

¾ teaspoon salt

2 tablespoons of olive oil, for oiling the baking sheet

coarse sea salt, for sprinkling

**For the pesto:**

100 g/3 cups fresh basil

6 garlic cloves

pinch of salt

90 ml/6 tablespoons olive oil

23 x 30-cm/9 x 12-inch baking sheet

Makes 1 loaf

Mix all the sponge ingredients together to form a thick batter. Cover with a clean wet towel and let sit in a warm place for 1 hour. Add the remaining ingredients to form a soft dough. Place on a clean work surface and knead for at least 5 minutes, adding extra flour when necessary. Form the dough into a ball. Place in an oiled mixing bowl, cover with a wet towel and let rise in a warm place for 2 hours.

Punch the dough down with a closed fist to release the trapped air.

Oil a baking sheet and then spread the dough out in a rectangular shape. Cover the baking sheet and let the dough rise for another hour.

Preheat the oven to 220°C (425°F) Gas 8. Make dimples in the dough by poking it with clean fingertips. Drizzle the dough with olive oil and sprinkle with coarse sea salt. Lower the heat to 200°C (400°F) Gas 6 and bake for 30–35 minutes in the preheated oven until golden brown. Carefully tap the bottom of the loaf to check if it's done – if it sounds hollow, it's ready. If not, bake for a couple more minutes at the bottom of the oven, if necessary.

To make the pesto, blend all the ingredients in a blender (or by using a pestle and mortar) into a thick paste; some leaf chunks are fine. Top the warm focaccia with the freshly made pesto just before serving, or serve the pesto on the side, as a dip.

# Double spelt & kefir bread

To make this bread I use both spelt flour and spelt sprouts or sprouted spelt, but it's the fizzy kefir that makes the bread rise so well. You could sprout some extra berries when sprouting for rejuvelac (see pages 24–25) so you have them ready to fold in, and in case you've recently made kefir cream cheese (see pages 26–27) use leftover whey in this recipe, instead of kefir. Nothing should go to waste!

450 g/3½ cups spelt flour (freshly milled, if possible)

10 g/2 teaspoons aluminium-free baking powder

1½ teaspoons salt

2 tablespoons olive oil

**480 ml/2 cups Milk Kefir (see pages 22–23)**

55 g/½ cup sprouted spelt

450-g/1-lb. (23 x 12 cm/6 x 4 inch) loaf pan lined with parchment paper (to fit inside without any creases)

oven thermometer (optional)

Makes about 14 slices

Preheat the oven to 220°C (425°F) Gas 8.

Whisk together the flour with the baking powder and salt. Add the olive oil and kefir and stir vigorously with a spatula until you get a smooth, thick batter. Fold in the sprouts.

Spoon the dough into the prepared loaf pan and make sure that it is level.

Put the pan into the preheated oven. Lower the temperature to 200°C (400°F) Gas 6 and bake for 1 hour. Use an oven thermometer if you're not sure about the exact temperature in the oven. If the temperature is below 200°C (400°F) Gas 6, the bread will not rise properly.

Remove the loaf pan from the oven, tip the bread out immediately, peel off the paper and allow to cool completely on a wire rack. This will prevent the bread from absorbing moisture and will keep the crust crisp. Wrap the bread in a tea/dish towel and store in a cool, dry place for up to 4 days.

# Cecina (Baked chickpea pancake)

An Italian-style baked chickpea pancake, cecina, makes a nice snack or light lunch together with a glass of chilled yogurt or kefir. It can be cut up in pieces and served as an appetizer with dips, salads or stews – it's a very versatile and tasty gluten-free and protein-rich pancake!

To make the cecina batter, whisk together the flour and yogurt or kefir whey, cover and let ferment for 6–10 hours. Add the salt and pepper.

Preheat the oven to 200°C (400°F) Gas 6.

With a silicone brush, oil an ovenproof frying pan/skillet with 1 tablespoon of olive oil. Put the pancake pan in the oven, and once hot, remove the pan and carefully pour in the cecina batter. Add 1 tablespoon of oil on top of the batter and gently whisk with a fork. Put back in the oven and bake for 22–25 minutes.

Cecina should have a thin, crispy outside and a softer, creamy inside when done. Grill/broil for the last 3 minutes to form a crust, if necessary. Flip out of the pan and serve hot, warm or cold.

120 g/¾ cup chickpea flour

360 ml/1½ cups yogurt whey or kefir whey (see pages 26–27)

2 tablespoons olive oil

salt and pepper, to taste

26–28-cm/10–11-in. ovenproof cast iron pancake pan

Serves 2

# Red lentil dosas

In case you have never tried to make fermented pancakes out of any type of beans or lentils, this is an easy recipe for total beginners. Except for the soaking and fermenting time, the process is pretty much the same as for any other pancakes – once the batter is ready they are fried in a little oil until lovely and golden brown.

200 g/1 cup red lentils

200 g/1 cup millet

¼ teaspoon sea salt

½ teaspoon crushed black pepper

¼ teaspoon ground turmeric

3 tablespoons chopped spring onions/scallions or fresh flat-leaf parsley

sesame oil, for frying

Makes 12–14

Wash the lentils and the millet. Cover with hot water and let soak for 8 hours. Drain, keeping the soaking water.

In a high-speed blender, blend the lentils and millet adding just enough of the soaking water to get a thick and smooth batter. Transfer into a bowl, cover with clingfilm/plastic wrap and let ferment in a warm place for 12–24 hours. The batter is ready when bubbles start forming on the surface. At this point, whisk in the remaining ingredients.

Heat a frying pan/skillet and use a pastry brush to cover it with a little oil. Pour a small ladleful of the batter into the pan/skillet and tilt the pan to spread the batter evenly. Once the edges start turning golden brown, flip the pancake over.

Dosas are best served warm with different types of cream cheese (see pages 94 and 97), with a hot condiment (see pages 118–119) or with a nice chutney. They can also be served with soups and stews, in place of bread.

# Grilled corn cake

This is a fantastic way to prepare and serve polenta, with the polenta turning delightfully creamy if it is left to soak in water. Any spices can be added, so feel free to experiment! Once cooled, the polenta is cut into thick slices and grilled/broiled before serving, for an additional smoky aroma. You can also skip this step and serve it without grilling/broiling.

Soak the polenta in water for about 48 hours. You'll know that it's fermenting when small bubbles start to appear. At this point, pour in a heavy-bottomed saucepan and bring to a slow boil, whisking vigorously. Add salt, paprika and oregano and stir for a bit longer. Lower the heat to a minimum, cover and let sit for 10 minutes. Remove from the heat, cover, and allow to sit for another 10 minutes before stirring well and adding the olive oil.

Oil the loaf pan – the size of the pan isn't that important since you can simply spoon polenta in one corner if the loaf pan is too big. Add the polenta and even out with a spatula or moist hands. The 'loaf' should be 5–6 cm/2–2½ inches thick. Let cool completely, then turn out to a clean work surface. With a sharp wet knife, carefully cut 1-cm/⅜-inch thick slices. Brush each slice with olive oil on both sides and place under a hot grill/broiler; it's best when charcoal or a gas grill is used, but a grill pan works too. Serve instead of bread or as a side dish for goulashes, stews or fish.

170 g/1 cup polenta/coarse cornmeal

600 ml/2½ cups water

¾ teaspoon sea salt

½ teaspoon sweet paprika

½ teaspoon dried oregano

4 tablespoons olive oil, plus extra for grilling/broiling

450-g/1-lb. loaf pan

Makes 1 x 450-g/1-lb. loaf

chapter six
# Condiments,
# dressings & dips

# Onion anchovies

These salty and aromatic strips of onion with a taste reminiscent of salted anchovies are a great little condiment to complement milder-tasting dishes and a good addition to spring rolls (see pages 84–85).

Peel the onions and slice in half lengthwise. Place each half round-side down, and start slicing 3–4 mm/⅛–inch thick half-moons, starting from the middle of the onion outwards. This way most of the sliced half-moons will stick together at one end and, in most cases, the layers won't divide.

Cover the bottom of the container with one-third of the miso. Place a layer of onion slices on top. Cover with another one-third of miso and even it with a small spatula, so that all the slices are covered in miso on all sides. Repeat with another layer of onions and the remaining miso. Makes sure all onions are covered. Cover the container and let sit at room temperature. It will take the onion 4 weeks to ferment into a mild and slightly sweet condiment.

As soon as the onion is taken out of the miso, wipe it or rinse quickly under running water, and serve. Slices taken out of the miso do not last longer than a couple of days in the fridge, so keep the remaining onion slices submerged in miso. After 1 month, place the container in the fridge. Use within a month.

2 large red onions (around 280 g/10 oz. total weight)

300 g/1¼ cups miso paste (I use garlic and red pepper miso in this recipe, but barley or rice miso also works well)

18 x 18-cm/5 x 5-in. glass container, with lid

# Garlic condiment

This is a delicious way to prepare and serve garlic. The fermentation process reduces its pungent taste and strong odour, making it more acceptable to eat daily without the fear of garlic breath!

Peel the garlic cloves. Boil a small saucepan of water and blanch the cloves, immersing them in boiling water for only 1–2 minutes. Drain. Cover the bottom of the container with miso. Add a layer of garlic cloves and cover with miso again. Repeat until all the ingredients are used. Cover tightly. Let sit in a cool place.

The mildest and nicest flavour is reached after 4 weeks of fermentation, although they'll still be tasty after only 6 days. Take the garlic cloves out of the miso, wipe and store in the fridge, tightly covered. Serve as an appetizer, as a condiment or crush and add to soups or stews just before serving.

10 garlic bulbs (around 500 g/ 18 oz. total weight)

300 g/1 cup barley or rice miso

# Turmeric & chilli kimchi

This is just one of many variations of the South Korean phenomenon kimchi. Take a spoonful or two every day with your main meal to improve digestion. It's worth making plenty at once and using it up within 2 months.

1.2 litres/6 cups cold water

60 g/3 tablespoons sea salt

600 g/7 cups green cabbage, cut into thick strips

8 carrots (around 520 g/1 lb. 3 oz. (total weight), cut into bite-sized pieces

20-g/¾-oz. piece fresh ginger

4 garlic cloves

4 small whole red chillies/chiles

1 teaspoon turmeric powder

½ teaspoon chilli powder

pickle press (optional)

Makes 300–400 g/3–4 cups

Make a brine by mixing the water and salt and stir well.

Put the cabbage and carrots into the pickle press (if using) and cover with the brine. To keep it submerged, screw the lid down just a little. Allow to soak for few hours or overnight. If you don't have a pickle press, put the vegetables in a bowl and weigh them down by resting a plate on top of them. Meanwhile, finely chop the ginger and garlic. Drain the soaked vegetables, reserving the brine. Mix them with the spices and add the chillies/chiles.

Put this mixture back into the pickle press or bowl and add enough brine to rise over the vegetables once you press them down. Screw the lid as much as you can, or, if using a plate, put something heavy on top of it. The vegetables must be submerged in the brine the entire time during fermentation. Check every 2 days and remove any foam or mould spots that might appear on the surface of the brine, which is totally normal. Allow to ferment for a minimum of 1 week but the best taste develops after 4 weeks. When the vegetables are done, transfer into jars, cover with the brine and keep in the fridge.

# Spicy leek & miso condiment

This condiment isn't just tasty, it's good for you, too! Leek, onions and garlic are well known for their therapeutic properties, and if you add olive oil, chilli and miso paste, you will get an aromatic blend rich in probiotics that will strengthen your immune system.

2 medium leeks
2 medium onions
1 garlic bulb, cloves crushed
5 tablespoons olive oil
1 small dried chilli, crushed
**1–2 tablespoons barley or rice miso**

Makes 200–300 g/2–3 cups

Slice the leeks in half lengthwise and wash thoroughly. Peel the onions and garlic and then finely chop all of the vegetables. Heat the oil in a heavy-based saucepan, and add the finely chopped leek and onion and a pinch of salt. Combine well and cover. Simmer over a low heat until the onion becomes translucent, about 20 minutes, stirring occasionally. Add the chilli and sauté for another minute. Meanwhile, dilute the miso in a little hot water in a bowl.

Remove the saucepan from the heat source (this is important since with boiling, healthy enzymes are destroyed), add the diluted miso and crushed garlic cloves and mix well. Add a little more hot water to reach the desired consistency. This condiment is quite sharp and salty – a spoonful of it per day is enough. It's a great addition to grain porridges and/or boiled vegetables. It will keep in the fridge for at least 1 week.

# Rich miso-tofu dressing

This dressing stays fresh in the fridge for days and adds some extra protein from tofu into your salad or snack. I love to use leftovers as a dip for raw vegetables and crackers, or as a bread spread.

200 g/1 cup fresh tofu
**2 teaspoons barley or rice miso**
4 teaspoons lemon juice
2 teaspoons Dijon mustard
3 teaspoons dark sesame oil
½ teaspoon salt
2 tablespoons finely chopped onion
60 ml/¼ cup water

Makes 320 g/1½ cups

Blend all the ingredients well until the mixture reaches a velvety consistency. Serve immediately or let sit in the fridge overnight before using. Add more water if you prefer a less dense dressing.

# Cashew mayonnaise dressing

I love any kind of home-made vegan mayonnaise and I did share some secrets in my previous book, *The Vegan Pantry*. Any vegan mayonnaise can be turned into a dressing simply by adding more liquid and blending it in. This type of dressing goes well with almost anything, and the fact that it contains nuts and seeds (and all of the good oils that they possess) makes it very satisfying. Use in salads, sandwiches or as a dip for raw vegetables.

Soak the nuts and seeds together overnight in the water with ¼ teaspoon salt. Drain, discard the liquid and rinse.

Put the soaked nuts and seeds in the blender with all other ingredients and blend until completely smooth – only a high-speed blender can achieve the velvety smoothness needed for this dressing! If it's too thick, add more rejuvelac to reach the desired consistency.

Cover and let sit at room temperature for 6–8 hours to ferment a bit more and to allow the flavours to develop.

90 g/⅔ cup unsalted cashews

85 g/⅔ cup sunflower seeds

720 ml/3 cups water, for soaking

3 tablespoons olive oil

1 teaspoon sea salt

4 tablespoons Rejuvelac
(see pages 24–25 )

1 soft date

180 ml/¾ cup cold water

1 tablespoon freshly squeezed
lemon juice

2 garlic cloves (optional)

Makes 400 g/1⅔ cups

# Ayvar (red-hot chilli sauce)

Vegetables for hot sauces and relishes are usually fried, baked or cooked with oil and vinegar before being blended into a liquid or a thick paste that is used in cooking or served with other foods. A great example of this is Ayvar, a delicious roasted red pepper relish worshipped in almost every Eastern European kitchen – the following recipe is its fermented incarnation. The fermentation process helps to develop an amazingly complex flavour.

3 medium red (bell) peppers (around 330 g/12 oz. total weight)

6 long green (or red) hot peppers, (around 140 g/5 oz. total weight)

2 onions (around 200 g/7 oz. total weight)

5 garlic cloves

1½ teaspoons salt

Makes 350 g/1½ cups

Remove the stems and seeds from all the peppers, wash well and pat dry. Slice the peppers and onions into thin slices. Use a garlic press to crush the garlic. Put all the ingredients into a bowl, add the salt and squeeze with clean hands until they start to 'sweat'. It is wise to use disposable gloves if the hot peppers are very hot, or your hands might burn!

Transfer this mixture into a wide-necked jar and pack it tightly (use a pestle or a similar object to do this). The liquid should rise above the vegetables. Place a small plate (that fits into the jar) on top of the vegetables and press down with something heavy (like a bottle filled with water or a stone) to keep the vegetables submerged. Cover with a clean tea/dish towel and let ferment at room temperature for a couple of weeks. Check every other day and remove any foam or mould that might appear.

When the fermentation process has done its job, drain the vegetables (keep the brine) and put in a blender or food processor. Blend into a smooth paste and keep adding the brine little by little until reaching the desired consistency. This hot sauce can be added at the end of cooking to spice up many dishes, or it can be served at the table as a condiment for those who like things hot!

# Tzatziki dip

I fell in love with this tangy cucumber dip while living in Greece, and I've been making it for more than a decade as soon as the cucumber season starts in the summer! Even though it can be made with store-bought yogurt, it's much tastier when using fresh, home-cultured yogurt. I like a rich and creamy tzatziki, and I achieve this by straining the yogurt to drain off some of the whey, as well as being careful to grate and salt the cucumbers beforehand and squeeze out as much cucumber juice as possible to prevent the dip becoming watery. It's a perfect complement to grilled vegetables and Pesto Focaccia (see pages 98–99) and can also be used as a salad dressing.

2 cucumbers (around 450 g/1 lb. total weight)

480 ml/2 cups strained home-made yogurt (see right)

6 tablespoons extra virgin olive oil

3 garlic cloves, crushed

2 tablespoons fresh chives, chopped/snipped

freshly squeezed lemon juice, to taste

sea salt and freshly ground black pepper, to taste

Makes 650 g/3 cups

To strain the yogurt, follow the instructions in the recipe for yogurt cream cheese (pages 26–27), but strain it only for 2 hours, or until it reaches the consistency you like.

Peel the cucumbers, cut them lengthwise and remove the seeds. Grate using a cheese grater. Put the grated cucumbers in a sieve/strainer; add a pinch of salt, mix and let drain for 20 minutes. Squeeze with your hands to remove the remaining juice and transfer into a bigger bowl. Add the strained yogurt and all the remaining ingredients. Mix well. Taste and adjust the seasoning, if necessary.

Tzatziki can be served straight away but is much tastier when refrigerated for several hours or overnight, allowing the flavours to blend. Feel free to use fresh dill, basil, parsley, mint or spring onions/scallions instead of chives, if you like. Drizzle with a little more olive oil just before serving and decorate with a few more fresh herbs. Tzatziki will keep in the fridge for up to 5 days.

chapter seven
# Probiotic drinks

# Very pink yogurt smoothie

This is a super-simple smoothie recipe made with only three basic ingredients. You can always make it a bit more filling if you like, by adding 1 tablespoon of either chia seeds, almond butter or nuts. I like it light, refreshing, a little more on the sour side. Add more dates if you like it sweeter!

In a high-speed blender, blend all ingredients until silky smooth. If you're using frozen fruit, thaw in advance. In summer, for a cool and refreshing smoothie, frozen fruits can be blended in directly.

A purple smoothie can be made by substituting raspberries or sour cherries with blueberries or blackberries; while a green version can be made adding one apple and 120 ml/½ cup green juice (made out of kale, chard, spinach, etc.). If you'd like a taste of the tropics, blend in mango, pineapple or papaya!

**480 ml/2 cups Yogurt (see pages 18–19)**

130 g/1 cup raspberries or stoned/pitted sour cherries

60 g/2 oz. (approximately 6) Medjool dates, stoned/pitted

Serves 2

# Coconut kefir smoothie

Fermented coconut water can be enjoyed by itself, but made into a delicious smoothie like this one, it's even tastier. I add coconut milk for a kick of coconut flavour, and while mango pairs wonderfully both in terms of taste and colour, other ripe and sweet fruits can be used too!

Put the water kefir grains in the jar, add the coconut water and stir well. Cover it loosely or seal with the jar lid (I prefer sealing the jar to get more fizziness). Keep the jar away from direct sunlight and leave to ferment for 2 days, stirring a couple of times in those 48 hours. Taste the liquid – it should taste more sour than sweet. Strain the liquid into a blender jar, add the coconut milk and the mango flesh and blend until completely smooth. Taste and add a little maple, rice or agave syrup as necessary.

This probiotic smoothie can also be made with pineapple, strawberries or peaches. In hot weather, add some ice chips before blending.

**2 tablespoons Water Kefir (see pages 20–21)**

480 ml/2 cups coconut water

240 ml/1 cup full-fat coconut milk

1 fully ripe mango (approximately 340 g/12 oz) or other ripe and sweet fruit

**maple, rice or agave syrup (optional)**

1-litre/34-fl. oz. preserving jar with tight-fitting lid

plastic strainer

wooden or plastic spoon

Serves 2

# Rehydration tonic

This is a real thirst quencher – it's very bubbly too! All the ingredients have a rehydrating effect on the body, and the fermentation adds enzymes to help your digestive system work optimally.

2 cucumbers (around
    400 g/14 oz. total weight)

2 yellow grapefruit (around
    600 g/1⅓ lbs. total weight)

240 ml/1 cup coconut water plus
    1 tablespoon of raw cane sugar
    OR 240 ml/1 cup water and
    4 tablespoons raw cane sugar

2 celery stalks/ribs (around
    140 g/5 oz. total weight)

6 mint or lemon balm (melissa)
    sprigs

**3 tablespoons Water Kefir
(see pages 20–21)**

1-litre/32-oz. preserving jar with lid

Serves 2

Wash the cucumbers and leave the skin on if they are organically grown. If not, peel them. Cut into pieces that will fit through a juice feeder.

Peel and cut the grapefruit into chunks. Wash and cut the celery stalks/ribs. Rinse the mint or lemon balm sprigs and pat dry. Pass all ingredients through a juicer (you should get about 720 ml/3 cups of juice). Pour the juice into the preserving jar and add either the coconut water mixture or the water mixture. Add the water kefir grains, close tight, shake well and let ferment at room temperature (should be above 20°C/68°F) for 2–3 days, until mildly sour and fizzy. Strain the juice and refrigerate before drinking.

You can rinse the kefir grains and re-use. You could also try using lemon instead of grapefruit and substitute cucumber with watermelon. Lettuce can also be used instead of celery, if you like.

# Strong ginger beer

If you like ginger beer and want to experience a real ginger kick, try this recipe! You couldn't fit more ginger taste into it even if you wanted to!

Peel and finely grate the ginger root. Put it in a heavy-bottomed saucepan. Add the water and sugar and cook over a low heat, stirring constantly for approximately 15 minutes, adding a little water if necessary to prevent burning. Strain through a fine-mesh sieve/strainer, squeezing out all the juice from the ginger. This is the ginger syrup you need to make strong beer.

Add 120 ml/½ cup of ginger syrup into the jar and pour over the pre-made ginger beer. Seal tightly and let ferment at room temperature for anything between a couple of hours to 2 days. Taste occasionally until the desired taste is reached. I like it fizzy and still quite sweet, but if you want a more alcoholic beverage, ferment it for longer!

**1-litre/quart Ginger Beer (see pages 30–31)**

**For the ginger syrup:**

450 g/1 lb. fresh ginger root

240 ml/1 cup water

130 g/⅔ cup raw cane sugar (muscovado or turbinado work best)

1.5-litre/48-oz. preserving jar with tight-fitting lid

Makes 1 litre/4 cups

# Mineral-rich beetorade

All the fruit and vegetables in this soda are full of different nutrients on their own, but combined, they make a powerful and energizing elixir. With a little help from the water kefir grains, which add many probiotics and enzymes to the mix, this beetorade becomes an explosion of flavour and nutrients!

7 small apples (around 800 g/1¾ lbs. total weight)

14 small carrots (around 1 kg/2¼ lbs. total weight)

6 oranges (around 780 g/14 oz. total weight)

1 beetroot/beet (approximately 200 g/6½ oz. in weight)

**5 tablespoons Water Kefir (see pages 20–21)**

2-litre/quart preserving jar with tight-fitting lid

Makes 1.5 litres/6 cups

Wash the apples, carrots and beetroot/beet. Cut into pieces that will fit through the feeder of your juicer. Peel the oranges and cut into sections. Pass everything through the juicer.

Pour the juice into the preserving jar, add the water kefir grains, mix well and seal the jar tightly. Allow to ferment for 24–48 hours, shaking occasionally to redistribute. Carefully open the jar after 24 hours of fermentation and taste. If it's already fizzy and slightly sour (bear in mind that fermentation is quicker during hot summer months), strain it and refrigerate for a couple of hours before drinking. If the soda isn't quite ready jet, let it ferment for another day before straining and refrigerating.

This is an amazing home-made soda with an enormous amount of vitamins, minerals and probiotics. Don't throw away the kefir grains – they will have turned orange or pink from sitting in the juice, but just rinse them under running water and feed with fresh juice or sweet water to keep them going.

# Apple cider

Water kefir grains will transform freshly squeezed apple juice into a cider in about four days and it's certainly worth the wait! I use a cold-press juicer which extracts a more nutritious juice from fruits and vegetables, but use any type of juicer you have. Alternatively, a 100 per cent natural, unsweetened and preferably organic, store-bought apple juice can also be used to make this cider.

Cut the apples into pieces that will fit through the feeder of the juicer and juice them. Pour the liquid into the preserving jar and add the kefir grains. Tightly seal the jar and let ferment for 2 days, shaking the jar twice a day. The grains will feed on the sugars within the fruit, so there's no need to add any extra sweetener.

After 48 hours carefully open the jar and strain the content through a plastic sieve/strainer into a bowl. Pick out and wash the kefir grains and re-use them to make a new batch of soda or cider. Wash, core and thinly slice the sweet apples for the second fermentation. Add them to the strained apple juice that should already be fizzy and tart from the first fermentation. Tightly close the jar and let sit at room temperature for another 24–48 hours. This will make it even more 'cidery'. Strain the content of the jar, seal and refrigerate for a couple of hours before drinking.

**Note:** In summer you might want to transfer the jar into the fridge for the second fermentation to prevent over-fermentation.

18 small organic apples, preferably crisp (around 2 kg/4½ lbs. total weight) or 1.2 litres/5 cups apple juice

**4 tablespoons Water Kefir (see pages 20–21)**

3–4 sweet apples (approximately 400 g/14 oz total weight), for the second fermentation

1.5 litre/quart preserving jar with tight-fitting lid

plastic strainer

wooden or plastic spoon

Makes 1.5 litres/6 cups

# Refreshing lemon & mint soda

This fizzy lemonade will forever change the way you think about soda! It's a hundred times tastier than all the commercial sodas out there. I especially enjoy drinking it chilled after my morning run during the warmer months of the year – it's so refreshing!

**4 tablespoons Water Kefir (see pages 20–21)**

100 g/½ cup raw cane sugar or other sweetener

1 litre/4 cups water, preferably non-chlorinated

1–2 organic lemons, peeled

handful of fresh mint leaves

1.5-litre/quart preserving jar with tight-fitting lid

plastic strainer

wooden or plastic spoon

1.5-litre/quart glass bottle or another 1.5-litre/quart preserving jar

Makes 1.5 litres/6 cups

Put the water kefir grains in the jar, add the sweetener and water and stir well. Cut each lemon into 8 slices and add to the jar together with the mint leaves. Seal with the jar lid. Keep the jar away from direct sunlight and leave to ferment for 2 days, stirring a couple of times in those 48 hours. Be careful when opening the jar because a considerable amount of carbon dioxide is produced by the fermentation!

Strain the liquid into a clean bottle or jar, squeeze out all the juice from lemon slices and add it, then discard the used lemon and mint leaves. Rinse the kefir grains and re-use. If you're not going to drink this soda right away, refrigerate and make sure it is well sealed to keep it fizzy.

# Real rice cream

Brown rice cream is very helpful when proper digestion is compromised. It is very nourishing without burdening the digestive system and a great meal for people who have problems with chewing, those with no appetite or those with a very troubled stomach. Rice cream cooked this way is healing and energizing; do not confuse it with powdered rice cream, which is a processed product and very different!

Wash and drain the rice, put it in a jar and cover with 240 ml/1 cup of water. Cover loosely with a lid and let ferment for 24–72 hours.

Put the rice with the soaking water in a pressure cooker; add the remaining 480 ml/2 cups of water and the umeboshi plum. Close the lid securely, bring to high pressure over a high heat, then transfer to the lowest heat possible and cook for 2 hours. Prepare a mesh strainer over a bigger bowl.

Allow the pressure to come down, open the lid and pour the rice into the strainer. Twist the pestle against the rice so that the rice cream passes through the strainer and you are left with slightly moist rice husks in the strainer. Discard the husks. In case you don't own a pressure cooker, use a heavy-bottomed saucepan with a heavy lid, and cook over very low heat for the same amount of time, but add another extra cup of water at the beginning of cooking.

It's best to consume fresh rice cream on the day you prepare it.

100 g/½ cup short-grain brown rice

720 ml/3 cups water

½ umeboshi plum, stoned/pitted

pressure cooker

double-mesh strainer

pestle

Serves 2

chapter eight
# Something sweet

# Berry no-cheese cheesecake

Creamy, cold, refreshing, slightly sour and a real looker, this no-cheese cheesecake is a lovely treat on hot summer days! My favourite fruit to use is sour cherries, but try the recipe with any berries or fruits that are in season, or any frozen fruits you might have in the freezer.

**For the topping:**

380 g/3 cups unsalted cashews

960 ml/4 cups water, for soaking

¼ teaspoon salt

120 ml/½ cup Rejuvelac (see pages 24–25) or 120 ml/½ cup Refreshing Lemon & Mint Soda (see pages 134–135) or water

200 g/⅔ cup rice, maple or agave syrup

150 ml/¾ cup virgin coconut oil, melted

freshly squeezed juice and grated zest of 2 organic lemons

240 g/2 cups frozen sour cherries

60 g/½ cup wild strawberries, fresh sour cherries or other berries

**For the crust:**

160 g/1 cup walnuts

60 g/½ cup dates

60 g/½ cup raisins

freshly squeezed juice and zest of 1 organic lemon

1 tablespoon rum or mirin (optional)

¼ teaspoon cinnamon

pinch of salt

20-cm/8 in. or 24-cm/10-inch cake pan, base lined with parchment paper

Serves 8–12

Soak the cashews in water and add ¼ teaspoon salt. This process will take 36 hours in summer and 72 hours in winter. They are ready when the water gets cloudy and a little sticky. Strain the cashews and wash thoroughly under running water.

To make the crust, process the walnuts in a food processor to get small chunks. Separately blend the raisins and dates into a paste with the lemon juice and zest, rum/mirin (if using), cinnamon and salt. In a bowl, combine the walnuts with the fruit paste to get a slightly sticky dough that holds together. Place the crust mixture into the prepared cake pan and distribute evenly with moistened hands. The crust will be quite thin, especially if you're using a 24-cm/10-inch cake pan, but that's alright. Refrigerate while making the topping.

To make the topping, blend the fermented and washed cashews with rejuvelac, soda or water to get a velvety-smooth cream. Add the syrup, melted coconut oil, lemon juice and zest and blend again until incorporated. Spoon one-third of this mixture on top of the prepared crust and push it with a spatula from the middle towards the sides. Add the frozen sour cherries to the remaining amount of cashew cream and blend again until smooth. Spoon onto the middle of the cake, leaving a thin edge of the bottom white cream all around the edge. Even the sour cherry cream with the spatula.

Sprinkle fresh berries on top and press gently into the cream. Place in the freezer for about 1 hour before serving, or until the cream is just right for cutting. Slice with a wet knife. Enjoy this refreshing raw cheesecake!

# Austrian-style kefir cheesecake

I rarely use eggs in baking, but this is a recipe where fresh egg whites are necessary to create a puffy and light topping. Traditionally served in Austrian-style coffee houses throughout central and Eastern Europe, this type of cheesecake is made with fresh farmer's cheese and sour cream. I use kefir and kefir cream cheese instead, which I think works fantastically well!

Preheat the oven to 180°C (350°F) Gas 4.

To make the crust, combine flour and salt, then fork in the cold butter until the mixture resembles coarse crumbs. Add the syrup and zest (and egg yolk, if using) and stir with a fork until well combined. Press the dough evenly into the prepared cake pan, forming a thin crust. Refrigerate for 15 minutes. Bake for about 12 minutes in the preheated oven, until lightly golden. Cool completely.

To make the topping, beat 4 egg whites with a handheld electric mixer until soft peaks form. Add 40 g/¼ cup raw brown sugar powder (or other brown sugar with a very fine consistency) and beat again until stiff peaks form. Set aside.

Beat the kefir cream cheese with kefir, remaining powdered sugar, vanilla, cornstarch, zest and salt until incorporated. Stir the raisins and one-third of the beaten egg whites into the cheese mixture, then gently fold in the rest of the whites. Pour over the crust and spread evenly. Bake in the preheated oven for about 40 minutes until the sides are somewhat puffed, and the surface of the cake is turning lightly golden. Do not overbake!

Even though the centre might still seem a little wobbly, it will set while cooling. Run a sharp knife or a cake spatula around the cake to release it. Let cool to room temperature. I love to eat this cheesecake while it's still warm; however, it is traditionally served completely chilled.

**For the crust:**

100 g/¾ cup chickpea/gram flour or millet flour (or wholemeal/whole-wheat flour)

⅛ teaspoon salt

1 egg yolk (optional)

100 g/7 tablespoons organic butter

1 tablespoon rice, maple or agave syrup

zest of 1 organic lemon

**For the topping:**

4 egg whites

80 g/½ cup raw brown sugar (blended into a powder using a blender), divided

580 g/2½ cups Kefir Cream Cheese (see pages 26–27)

240 ml/1 cup Milk Kefir (see pages 22–23)

½ teaspoon bourbon vanilla powder or 2 teaspoons pure vanilla extract, alcohol-free

grated zest of 3 organic lemons

2 tablespoons cornflour/cornstarch

¼ teaspoon salt

60 g/½ cup raisins

22-cm/8½-inch springform cake pan, base lined with parchment paper

Serves 8

# Melt-in-your-mouth sauerkraut brownies

So far, there's a brownie recipe in each of my cookbooks: Raw Brownies in *Raw Food Kitchen*, Bean and Cashew Brownies in *The Vegan Baker*, and brownies in the form of *Gooey Chocolate Cookies* in *The Vegan Pantry*. Well, what we have here are delicious brownies with sauerkraut! You won't believe how good they taste; the fermented cabbage is well hidden and adds an umami flavour without getting noticed!

**Liquid ingredients:**

120 ml/½ cup yogurt whey, kefir whey, milk kefir, water kefir, rejuvelac, plant milk or water (see note)

50 ml/¼ cup olive oil

150 g/½ cup maple, rice or agave syrup

¼ teaspoon bourbon vanilla powder

**85 g/½ cup Sauerkraut with Quinces (see pages 76–77), rinsed and chopped**

80 g/½ cup walnuts or other nuts, chopped

45 g/¼ cup dark/bittersweet chocolate, chopped

**Dry ingredients:**

130 g/1 cup unbleached plain/all-purpose flour

35 g/¼ cup wholemeal/whole-wheat flour

½ teaspoon bicarbonate of/baking soda

¾ teaspoon baking powder

30 g/⅓ cup cocoa powder

½ teaspoon cinnamon powder

24 x 18-cm/10 x 7-inch baking sheet, lined with parchment paper

Makes 12–15

Preheat the oven to 180°C (350°F) Gas 4.

In a large bowl, combine the chosen 120 ml/½ cup of liquid with the oil, syrup, vanilla and sauerkraut. Whisk well. Place a sieve/strainer on the top of the bowl and add the dry ingredients. Shake until sifted through. Whisk in both the liquid and dry ingredients to form a thick batter. Fold in the walnuts and chocolate.

Spoon into the prepared baking pan and bake for 25–27 minutes. Let cool and serve on its own, with apple sauce or with fresh berries.

**Note:** You can use yogurt whey (see pages 26–27), kefir whey (see pages 26–27), Milk Kefir (see pages 22–23), Water Kefir (see pages 20–21), Rejuvelac (see pages 24–25), any plant milk or even just plain water.

# Sweet cinnamon & yogurt scones

These rustic scones are an excellent way to use leftover home-made yogurt sitting in the fridge. Dried figs give them a Mediterranean touch, but feel free to substitute with any other dried fruits. Kefir can also be used, instead of yogurt, with equally yummy results. If you want to make vegan scones use soya/soy yogurt and non-hydrogenated margarine instead of butter. Also, use maple sugar or raw brown sugar if coconut palm sugar isn't available.

130 g/1 cup unbleached plain/
  all-purpose flour

60 g/½ cup wholemeal/
  whole-wheat flour

2 teaspoons baking powder

½ teaspoon cinnamon

¼ teaspoon bourbon vanilla
  powder

¼ teaspoon salt

45 g/⅓ cup pure coconut
  palm sugar

45 g/¼ cup butter

120 g/½ cup Yogurt
  (see pages 18–19)

90 g/⅔ cup dried figs

**For the cinnamon glaze:**

35 g/¼ cup pure coconut
  palm sugar

1 teaspoon ground cinnamon

1 tablespoon Yogurt
  (see pages 18–19)

baking sheet lined with parchment paper

Makes 10

Preheat the oven to 200°C (400°F) Gas 6.

Sift together the flours, baking powder, cinnamon, vanilla and salt in a bowl. Add the coconut sugar and whisk. Rub the butter into the dry ingredients until the mixture resembles fine breadcrumbs. Gently incorporate the yogurt and figs. Add an extra spoonful of yogurt if the mix seems overly dry. Divide the dough into 10 spoonfuls and drop onto the prepared baking sheet, leaving a little space between them. Pat down the tops to neaten them.

Combine the glaze ingredients until smooth. With the help of a pastry brush glaze the top of each scone. Bake in the preheated oven for 15–20 minutes. Allow to cool slightly on the baking sheet. Sprinkle some extra cinnamon and coconut sugar on just before serving with a little butter, and maybe a drizzle of maple syrup.

# Fritule

Fritule are sweet and fragrant deep-fried, free-form doughnut balls, a festive Croatian sweet made particularly for Christmas. I make them a couple of times a year when I want a comforting dessert that reminds me of childhood Christmases spent at my grandma's home in Istria. My version is somewhat different from the traditional recipe as I don't use eggs and add kefir/yogurt instead, which makes them lighter, so I'm able to eat a couple more fritule than I'm supposed to!

In a large bowl, whisk together the flours, sugar, yeast, salt and vanilla. Put the raisins in a small bowl and add the rum, the hot water and lemon zest. Let soak for 10 minutes.

Add the kefir, grated apple and raisins (together with the soaking liquid) to the bowl with the flour mixture and stir for a while with a spatula to get a sticky dough. Cover with a wet cloth and let sit in a warm place for 1–3 hours, until the dough doubles in size.

Add the oil in a small saucepan so the fritule can be deep-fried. Heat the oil until it starts moving. Drop a small piece of dough in it; if it starts to sizzle and lifts to the top immediately, it's ready. With an oiled spoon take a small ball of dough and drop it in the oil. Fry only 2–3 fritule at a time in order not to cool the oil. With a help of wooden chopsticks or a fork, turn each fritula to brown evenly on both sides. The right temperature of oil is crucial: if too hot, the fritule will burn and remain raw on the inside; if too cold, they will soak up a lot of oil and turn soggy. Drain each batch on paper towels.

Place all the fritule on a serving plate. Traditionally, icing/confectioners' sugar is used to sprinkle over fritule before serving, but I prefer grinding good-quality cane sugar and use that for sprinkling. Serve the fritule warm with a cup of rosehip or other tea. Leftovers can be kept in an airtight container for the next day.

175 g/1⅓ cups unbleached plain/all-purpose flour

45 g/⅓ cup wholemeal/whole-wheat flour

1 tablespoon raw brown sugar or coconut palm sugar

1 teaspoon active dry yeast

¼ teaspoon salt

¼ teaspoon bourbon vanilla powder

4 tablespoons raisins

½ tablespoon rum

2 tablespoon hot water

grated zest of 1 organic lemon

**180 ml/¾ cup yogurt whey or kefir whey (see pages 26–27)**

1 apple, peeled and grated

240 ml/1 cup oil, for frying

a little ground raw sugar, for sprinkling

Makes about 15

# Istrian supa

This is a fantastic recipe to share, and since the two basic ingredients are made with the help of fermentation, it fits perfectly into this cookbook! In my version of supa, the main ingredients are Teran red wine (a speciality of Croatia), sourdough bread and honey. Some people consider it to be a wine soup and some think of it as a dessert; I add a good share of honey to neutralize the somewhat acidic taste of the Teran wine so when served at my home we think of it as a sweet. Istrian supa is served in a special ceramic jug called a *bukaleta* and enjoyed between family and friends by the fireplace, passed from person to person until it's all gone. There is a saying: *The bread took all the wine and made me drunk!* so be careful!

1 litre/4 cups Teran red wine, or any hearty rustic red wine with good acidity

4 tablespoon of raw honey (my favourite to use for supa is black locust honey)

1 tablespoon of extra virgin olive oil

pinch of sea salt

pinch of freshly ground black pepper

**4 slices of sourdough bread (see pages 36–37), preferably grilled or well toasted**

Serves 4

Heat the wine until warm. Add honey, olive oil, salt and pepper and whisk until the honey dissolves completely. Pour into a ceramic jug.

Pieces of toasted bread are either added to the warm wine before serving and the supa is eaten with a spoon, or each person takes one slice of bread and dips it into the wine, sipping more wine with every bite. Enjoy the scent and taste of ancient times!

# Probiotic pumpkin popsicles

This is a great way to use pumpkin when in season; it's so delicious when used raw, even though few people experiment with uncooked squash or pumpkin, which is a real shame! I'm offering you a very simple and mild popsicle recipe; however, any smoothie or juice can be made into a popsicle, so unleash your imagination!

Strain the soda, squeeze the juice out of the soaked lemon and discard the lemon and mint pieces. In a high-speed blender, blend the pumpkin or squash cubes with the soda, agave syrup and lemon juice until velvety smooth. Taste and adjust the amount of syrup and lemon to taste (the sweetness highly depends of the type of pumpkin used).

Pour into popsicle moulds and freeze. Carefully remove from the mould by holding the handle and gently pulling out the popsicle. Eat immediately!

480 ml/2 cups **Refreshing Lemon & Mint Soda (see pages 134–135)**

240 g/2 cups **raw pumpkin or squash flesh, cubed**

2 tablespoons **agave syrup**

2 tablespoons **lemon juice**

12 popsicle moulds
(60 ml/2 fl. oz each)

Makes 12

# Sources & Resources

## Sources for fermentation equipment

www.kefirshop.co.uk – supplier of kefir, kombucha, ginger beer plant and more

www.fusionteas.com – excellent source of good quality milk kefir grains and kombucha mothers.

www.culturesforhealth.com – starters, kits, kitchen appliances, etc.

www.gemcultures.com – starters for milk kefir, kombucha, bread leavens, water kefir, etc.

www.amazon.com – The Kitchen & Home department offers fermentation crocks, tall glass bottles, mason jars, nut milk bags, mesh strainers, funnels, cotton muslin/cheesecloths, different types and sizes of Japanese pickle presses etc.

www.i herb.com great source of good-quality ingredients with affordable prices and small shipping costs to Europe

www.sauerkrautpots.com – based in The Netherlands, this company supplies fermenting crocks, graters, pounders and more.

## Internet resources about fermentation

www.culturesforhealth.com – articles, videos, recipes and more on fermentation

www.livingcultures.wordpress.com – fermentation as a social imagination project by artist Eva Bakkeslett

www.wildfermentation.com by Sandor Ellix Catz

## Books about fermentation

Andoh, Elizabeth. *Kansha: Celebrating Japan's Vegan and Vegetarian Traditions.* Berkeley, CA: Ten Speed Press, 2010.

Catz, Sandor Ellix. *The Art of Fermentation: An In-depth Exploration of Essential Concepts and Processes from Around the World.* White River Junction, VT: Chelsea Green Publishing, 2012.

Catz, Sandor Ellix. *Wild Fermentation: The Flavour, Nutrition and Craft of Live-Culture Foods.* White River Junction, VT: Chelsea Green Publishing, 2003.

Fallon, Sally. *Nourishing Traditions: The Book that Challenges Politically Correct Nutrition and the Diet Dictocrats.* Brandywine, MD: NewTrends Publishing, Inc., 2001.

Hisamatsu, Ikuko. *Tsukemono: Japanese Pickling Recipes.* Tokyo: Japan Publications, 2005.

Kushi, Michio and Marc Van Cauwenberghe. *Macrobiotic home remedies: Your Guide to Traditional Healing Techniques.* New York: Square One Publishers, 2007.

Ruppenthal, R.J. *How to make Probiotic Drinks for a Raw Food Diet.* CreateSpace Independent Publishing Platform, 2012.

Schinner, Miyoko. *Artisan Vegan Cheese: From Everyday to Gourmet.* Summertown, TN: Book Publishing Company, 2012.

Shurtleff, William and Akiko Aoyagi. *The Book of Miso: Food for Mankind.* New York: Ballantine Books, 1981.

# Index

# Acknowledgements

Since my dad Branko Gulin introduced me to the fascinating world of fermentation, I have to thank him first! Also, thanking my husband, family and best friends for their continuous support is an absolute must in each and every one of my cookbooks.

I want to use this opportunity to thank my students and workshop participants who have been following my work throughout the years, investing their time and money and trusting that I will teach them something interesting and useful on every occasion. I'm especially thankful that they all showed such an interest in my fermentation experiments, which resulted in this cookbook! These beautiful people, most of them women, come from all parts of Croatia and they are the ones who motivate me to go on and delve further into the world of healthy cooking and food preparation; they are the ones whose opinions matter the most! A big thank you goes to:

Nela Orač, Kristina Ibrahimović, Lidija Banai, Saša Cestar, Anja Grubiša, Ivana Cicarelli, Dorotea Solomun, Marijana Cigrovski, Mirjana Hanzec, Marina Demšić, Lina Šojat, Višnjica Habdija, Ira Galić, Renata Krivohlavek, Danijela Cerin, Ljiljana Pranjić, Tina Bilić, Marijana Dugandžić Cvetko, Darja Gavočanov, Sandra Pilat, Tamara Iharoš, Olivera Damijanić, Nataša Vrsaljko Alić, Iva Tominović Matas, Mia i Roberta Berneš, Cvetka Celija, Ljilja Čanković, Sonja Boljun, Viviana Celija, Klara Benko, Iva Jarec, Eufemija Franja, Altea Beletić, Mateja Medić, Sanja Jurić, Jadranka Spudić, Darija Buljan, Vesna Rikić, Tamara Ivančić, Gracijela i Lorena Golob, Ivona Mladineo, Anita Bubić, Ljubica Šare Vrdoljak, Mirjana Fingerhut, Sanja Ugarković, Ornela Bundalo Lukina, Jasna Sačić, Branka Kos, Nina Novotni, Anamarija Pogorelec, Dunja Floričić, Ines Dobrović, Sandra Blažević, Vesna Kurilić, Zvezdana Galić, Zorana Mavrić Korošec, Deniza Darlić, Sabina Šinkovec, Zlata Kanurić and all those whose names I might have forgotten to put on this list but they surely deserve to be on it. Thank you for sharing this wonderful food journey with me!